MAKING IDEAS
MATTER

My Life as a Policy Entrepreneur

━━━━━━━━ ∞ ━━━━━━━━

REPRESENTATIVE
DWIGHT EVANS

with William Ecenbarger

ೞ

Making Ideas Matter by
Representative Dwight Evans

Books may be purchased in quantity and/or
special sales by contacting the publisher,
Fels Institute of Government at the University of Pennsylvania.

All profits from the sale of this book will benefit the Fels
Institute of Government at the University of Pennsylvania.

Published by:
Fels Institute of Government at the University of Pennsylvania,
Philadelphia, PA

Designed and Edited by: KivaFresh

ISBN: 978-0615909080

FIRST EDITION

Cʒ

Dedication
To my grandmother, Katherine Odoms,
and to citizen Charity Buchanan,
both of whom demanded
the best from me.

ભ

Acknowledgements

This book would not have been possible without the support and encouragement of many people. David Haas and the Philadelphia Foundation believed in my idea; David Thornburgh and Lauren Cristella, at the Fels Institute of Government, made it possible; and Pulitzer Prize winner William Ecenbarger and researcher Tess Mullen shaped 30 years of government and politics into readable prose. Any mistakes or omissions are my fault, not theirs.

I owe so much more than a simple thank you to my mother, Jean Evans, and my siblings Linda, Henry, Duane and Gary; my grandfather, Bernard Odoms, Sr.; and my uncle, Bernard Odoms. Over the years many people worked tirelessly in my Philadelphia and Harrisburg offices; I salute them for their public service. In particular I want to thank Kimberly Turner, Linda Ford, Phyllis Benson, Lisa Renee Hendrickes, Zenobia Waridi, and Johnna Pro. On the campaign side, my first supporters were the residents of Homer Street, most especially, Alice 'Cookie' Colon, Arthur Satchell, and Louise and Louis George. Ora Love started it all with my initial campaign kick-off in 1980; Evangeline Rush delivered the first of many victories, and Mary Jane Wiggins kept me on track.

The late Fannie B. Burrows was one of many teachers who had a powerful influence on me, and her work lives on through thousands of students whom she taught at the Robert M. Fulton Elementary School. Norma Eley, Lafayette Barnes and Ron Pugh were mentors early on, and I value all that they taught me. I admire the work, commitment, and entrepreneurial spirit of Beverly Harper and Aurelia Saunders.

I offer my sincere gratitude to the following people for their wise counsel and their friendship over many years: Robert Archie, Nolan Atkinson, Terri Grantham, Ernest Jones, Jack Kitchen, Rhonda Lauer, Joe McLaughlin, Tom Muldoon, John Myers, Cherelle Parker, Melonease Shaw, Carl Singley, Ralph Smith, Terri Stigler, Marian Tasco, Sharmain Matlock-Turner, Jake Wheatley and Herman Wooden.

Finally, I want to thank the voters of the 203rd legislative district for giving me a chance to serve them in public office for 30 years. It has been a privilege.

Table of Contents

cȝ

CR

Foreword

There's a truism in the news business that nobody reads process stories—stories about how things happen, not just what happened or who did what to whom. Process stories are boring, and they certainly don't sell newspapers (or deliver Google Ad hits, or however people make money in journalism these days).

This is a process story and, worse, it's a process story about government, politics, and policy. But at the Fels Institute of Government at the University of Pennsylvania, we love process stories. In fact, for over 75 years we've been using process stories to teach emerging public leaders in our Masters in Public Administration program how to lead, how to manage, how to get things done.

I'd known PA State Representative Dwight Evans for a number of years when he called in 2011 to discuss his interest in writing a book with the Fels Institute of Government. I'd known him as a policy innovator, and a powerful political leader, mostly during my years as Executive Director of the Economy League of Greater Philadelphia, a business-led "think and do tank" in the region. I'd known he was instrumental in revitalizing Ogontz Avenue and West Oak Lane, in getting the Pennsylvania Convention Center built in the mid-90s, in championing school choice and effective policing in the late 90s, and in promoting

CR

better access to fresh food in urban areas. I also knew he'd been an unsuccessful candidate for "higher" office: Lt. Governor and Governor of Pennsylvania, twice for Mayor of Philadelphia.

I'll confess that I was, and am, an admirer of his. He had always showed a relentless curiosity, a glass half-full approach to life, and seemingly the (increasingly rare) ability to reach across party lines, and racial and economic divides, to bring people together to make things better for the people he represents.

Nevertheless, as we talked about his book-writing interest I was a little concerned that he was proposing either a soft-focus "The Dwight Evans Story" hagiography or, less likely, a tell-all, behind-the-scenes story of how things "really work" in Harrisburg. It quickly became apparent that he had neither in mind, and that both of us—he a long-time player in the game of politics and me more observer, student, and sideline coach—shared an interest in telling a story— a process story—of how one man came to learn and practice the political arts necessary to turn an idea into a reality.

For those like us at Fels who try to inspire and educate future public leaders, there are not enough stories like this one, stories that give aspiring practitioners of public leadership a sense of what they're getting into, a sense that there's a difference between getting the right policy answer and leading others to that right answer. In our business, the art of public leadership balances what Dr. James Spady, my predecessor at Fels, liked to call the dual competencies: the technical competencies necessary to figure out the best answer to a public policy problem and the political competencies necessary to see them into reality.

Process stories about politics are not always pretty. In teaching political leadership at Fels, I've become a student and disciple

CB

of Robert Caro and his masterful works on the great public builder Robert Moses (*The Power Broker*) and Lyndon Johnson (4 volumes, 5,000 pages and counting!), arguably the most effective president of at least the 20th century. Moses and Johnson were not nice people (though both could be charming) and in the light of history made some bad, even indefensible, choices for their city and their country. But they knew how to get things done; as Caro quotes Lyndon Johnson in the preface to *Master of the Senate*: "I do understand power, whatever else may be said about me. I know where to look for it, and how to use it."

In this time of squawking and cynical political partisanship, coming to terms with the legitimate sources and uses of political power seems enormously important. How else can dreams be realized, cities transformed, great institutions built, without the willingness and ability of our men and women to learn how to become political leaders in the best sense of the words? Ideas are not self-executing; reports don't sit on shelves because they're bad reports. Things happen because people make them happen. "Power," in the words of feminist Gloria Steinem, "is taken, not given."

In working with Dwight Evans on this book (with the able assistance of Bill Ecenbarger, former Harrisburg Bureau Chief for the *Philadelphia Inquirer*—a great writer and a class act—and Tess Mullen, a remarkably capable 2013 Fels graduate.) I've come to appreciate even more the value and impact of his political leadership. For 30 years, Dwight has served his constituents, and the citizens of the Commonwealth, with energy, conviction, purpose, and a relentless sense that he can make a difference, that as a legislator (not mayor, governor, or president) he can find a way to make ideas matter. He is not without his faults, as none of us is without ours. But as a citizen of Philadelphia and Pennsylvania, I'm grateful to him for the example he sets for our students and other men and women who aspire to follow in his footprints.

David Thornburgh
Executive Director, Fels Institute of Government
October, 2013

Working-Class

I grew up in a working-class family in a working-class neighborhood. When I was a kid, everyone worked. My mom, my dad, my aunts, my uncles, my grandfathers, and my grandmother – everyone worked. My dad had a job with a moving and storage company, and my mom worked as a secretary and a waitress. As a little boy, I learned to do math by sitting on our living room floor and counting up the tips my mom brought home from her job at the restaurant at the Marriott Hotel on City Line Avenue. On a good night, my mom might earn $100. As I counted up those dollar bills, I knew that my mom had worked hard for every dollar she got.

In my family, work was more than a source of income. It was a source of dignity. I was proud of my pop because I knew that he was one of the best packers and movers at his company. I recently ran into my pop's old boss at a political event and the first thing he did when he saw me was smile and say, "You're Hank's son." I was proud of my mom too. Even as a little boy, I could see what a good waitress she was. She was constantly watching out for her customers and anticipating their needs. She knew how to read people, and she knew how to serve them well. Whatever my parents did, they did it with excellence.

My parents, Hank and Jean Evans, started out their life together in a rental home in North Philadelphia. My big brother

Henry was born in 1949, and I was born in 1954. Then came my little sister Linda and my two younger brothers, Duane and Gary. Our North Philadelphia neighborhood was filled with families – my pop's mom and dad lived a block away, and his sister lived around the corner. Even if they weren't blood relatives, all of our neighbors looked out for me and my brothers and sister. Wherever we went, there was always someone there looking out the window to make sure we weren't getting into trouble.

As their family grew, my parents saved up to buy their own place in Philadelphia's Germantown neighborhood, which was a white, middle class neighborhood at this time. In 1959, they bought a three bedroom house on East Tulpehocken Street. We lived there for eight years until my parents separated in 1968. After that, my mom moved us to a house on Homer Street in West Oak Lane. My mother still lives in that house, and I have lived within a 15-minute walk of it ever since.

After my parents' separation, there continued to be structure in our house. Dinner was at five P.M., and if you didn't show up you went to your room hungry. You had to go to school, you had to do your homework, and you had to go to church on Sunday. Growing up, my family went to Providence Baptist Church for services, Sunday school and Wednesday Bible study. It was at Providence Baptist where I first read that well-known Bible verse from 1 Timothy 6:10 which says, "The love of money is the root of all evil." As I grew up, however, I made the distinction that it was the love of money, not money itself, that is the root of all evil. Money itself is nothing to be ashamed of. Indeed, it is hard to have dignity without it. If you used money well, you could do great and unselfish things.

As a child, I knew my mother was smart because she always

had the answers to our questions. One summer day when I was seven years old, she told me I was wasting too much time and I should go to the library. In my house, when Mom told you to do something, you did it. So I walked down the street and into a building that would soon become one of my favorite spots. Once I started reading, I couldn't stop. I read everything I could get my hands on. I still read two or three books a month on average, mostly on policy issues and history. Reading has always been one of the keys to my success – it is one of the best ways I know of to find new solutions for old problems.

In addition to turning me into a reader, my mom always wanted to make sure I got the best possible education. When we moved to West Oak Lane, I started eighth grade at Wagner Junior High School. Wagner was very different from Roosevelt, where I had gone the year before. Roosevelt was safe and orderly. Wagner had two different gangs, and even as a young boy I could tell that it was unsafe. My mom was very worried that I wouldn't get the education I needed there, so she decided to do something about it.

The next spring, as she was filling out our school forms, my mom manipulated our home address so that I could go to a better school. In effect, my mom exercised her own version of school choice. At the time, I didn't know what she had done. All I knew was that the next year, I was in a better school with better teachers. I remember sitting in my ninth grade algebra class at Leeds Junior High School and thinking, "These teachers aren't kidding around. I'll have to work hard to make it here." The next summer I had to go to summer school just to keep up.

As I look back on what my mom did, I am filled with gratitude and anger. I am grateful that I had a mom who would

CR

do anything she could – even forge our address – to make sure I got a good education. But I'm mad that my mother had to lie to the government in order to ensure her child could go to a good school. Thirty years after my mom did this, in the mid-1990s, I pushed for legislation to help launch charter schools in Pennsylvania because I believe that all families should have choices when it comes to educating their children. While I didn't think about it at the time, today I realize in advocating for charter schools, I was trying to provide parents with the tools they needed to fight for their children, just like my mom fought for me.

My mom is a strong woman, and there is no doubt in my mind that she got a lot of her strength from her own mother. My grandmother, Katherine Odoms, was a powerful influence on me and my siblings. If we did anything wrong, she would just look at us and ask, "Is that right?" We always knew from her tone of voice that it wasn't. Grandma was the anchor, the center of gravity for our family. Since she got up early every morning to work as a seamstress, she decided she would be our very own alarm clock: Every morning she would call us to wake us up for school and to tell us to get at it.

My mother and grandmother ensured that I was grounded in the basic principles of right and wrong. As a state legislator, I have always fought for policies that could help give children – particularly low-income children – a better life. But while government has a role in caring for children, I've never forgotten that the family is the most important thing in a child's life. A safe and nurturing family environment is essential to happiness and productivity.

Even though my mom did everything she could to smooth the transition, my mom and pop's separation was still a turning point in my childhood. I was thirteen years old, and I knew I had to step up. My mom had four kids at home to take care of, and it wouldn't be easy. So I told my mom that she did not have to give me any more money: I would pay my own way from that moment on. I would buy my own lunch, my own clothes, and my own books. That was my pledge to her. I wanted to be one less burden on her. I never took a dime from her after that.

With that pledge, I went to work. I got my first job when I was fourteen. I had to lie about my age to get it because under child labor laws workers were supposed to be at least sixteen years old. I worked after school and on Saturdays in the kitchen at Rolling Hill Hospital for $1.10 an hour. The hospital was in the suburbs, and I had to travel forty-five minutes on three different buses to get there. My main job there was to take food carts up to the patients' floors so that someone could serve their meals to them. Then, after the meals were delivered, I would bring the food cart back down to the kitchen and clean the dishes. I eventually got to where I was supervising others.

I worked hard all through high school. I was in food service at three other hospitals. I shucked clams at a restaurant, worked the register at a convenience store, and did some heavy lifting at a mattress factory. Even though my jobs weren't easy, I loved working. Getting that paycheck and knowing that I didn't have to depend on my mother for money made me proud. After graduating from Germantown High School, I got a job at a garage door company, but I was laid off after a few months. That motivated me to go to college. I started at the Community College of Philadelphia and then transferred to La Salle University in the fall of 1973.

17

ଓଃ

As much as I liked to work, I also liked to have a good time. When I was eighteen and nineteen years old, I loved going to local night clubs to listen to music. I went to Impulse on Broad Street, Cyros on Ogontz Avenue, and other places all around the city. A lot of these clubs were owned by black entrepreneurs who were always trying to build a crowd for their events. One night, I looked out over the audience and thought to myself, "There's an opportunity to make money here." The club owners always wanted a good crowd, and I was confident I could get them one.

I decided that to help pay my way through college, I would become an event organizer. My strategy was simple: I arranged for a dinner, dance or disco at a local club and then sold tickets to it. The owners loved this setup, because hosting events helped them attract new customers. To build a crowd, I had a network of ticket sellers throughout the city. With the proceeds from our ticket sales, I paid the club's owner to offer everyone one or two free drinks. Any money that was left over after that, I kept. In return for their help, my ticket sellers got free admission to the event. I was just nineteen years old when I organized my first big event in 1973. Over the next few years, I developed a reputation, and my events built up a following. I also started to build political connections, because in those days these black-owned bars were centers of political fund-raising.

I started organizing events because I thought it would be a fun way to get tuition money. However, I got a lot more than money out of this experience. Through my ticket selling, I developed fund-raising, negotiating, and organizing skills that have been helpful throughout my public career. I learned how to build relationships with people with different incomes, educations, and occupations. I also learned that people like success, so it is important to keep building the momentum so that your team can take pride in being part of something good.

When I was selling tickets, I had to ask people for help, because I couldn't make my operation work without them. Fortunately, the truth is most people want to be helpful. The worst thing someone could tell me was no, and if they did, I never got offended. I'd just go ask someone else. I developed drive and fortitude – if I wanted to get something accomplished, I would just go ask. This practice has served me well, because one of the first rules of politics is that you must ask people to help you. In the state legislature, you'll never get anything done if you don't ask for others' support.

Once I had my ticket sellers lined up, the key was to keep them motivated. To do this, I always looked at what our relationship was – whether someone was a high school friend, college friend, or neighborhood buddy. Building from that, I would try to figure out what drove that person and how I could get him to share my goals. I had to really understand the people that I was dealing with. That has never changed. Whether it was a ticket seller or a governor, my question has always been, what will it take to get you to do what I want? Nine times out of ten, the answer is reasonable. Time and time again, I've seen that if you can really understand people's needs and then get them to share your vision, they will help you enact your plan.

I didn't sleep much during the 1970s. I was in college, I was organizing events, and I was getting deeply involved in community issues and politics. Growing up in the 1960s, I had seen great men and women taking action to change their country. One of the men who impressed and influenced me the most as I started to wade into politics myself was Reverend Leon Sullivan, a Philadelphia legend and civil rights hero.

Reverend Sullivan was a West Virginia-born Baptist minister who came to Zion Baptist Church in Philadelphia, where he became a great civil rights leader and social activist focused on job creation and job training. From a young age, I knew of Sullivan as a driving, positive force in the African-American community. The more I learned about him, the more I wanted to be like him. In 1959, Sullivan organized a boycott of Philadelphia businesses that had declined to interview young blacks for jobs. Using the slogan, "Don't Buy Where You Don't Work," the boycott was extraordinarily effective and resulted in thousands of job opportunities for African-Americans. Because of his success, Sullivan was contacted by Dr. Martin Luther King Jr., and this led directly to the Southern Christian Leadership Conference creating an economic arm that was headed by Jesse Jackson.

Sullivan knew that African-Americans needed better paying jobs if they were to overcome the barriers of poverty, and that job training was key. So he founded Opportunities Industrialization Centers (OIC) of America in a dilapidated, derelict jail in North Philadelphia. The OIC trained young men and women to meet Philadelphia businesses' employment needs. The results were remarkable, and the idea quickly spread to other cities.

What has always impressed me the most about Leon Sullivan is how he empowered people to change their own communities. It was Sullivan who came up with the 10-36 Plan, a program through which families agreed to invest $10 a month for thirty-six months in a community fund. The money was used for scholarships, health services, housing and economic development projects. As I read about this, two things struck me: People were willing to work hard to better themselves – and they needed money to do it.

In the late 1960s, Sullivan built Progress Plaza, America's first black-owned and black-developed shopping center. In his autobiography *Build Brother Build*, Sullivan recounts how he persuaded the city of Philadelphia to donate the land for the project and then raised money to build the center. "I went to the chairman of the bank and I said, 'I want a construction loan.' He said, 'Well, Reverend, you need some equity for something like this. Think about it and come back later in two, three or four years, and let's see what we can do.'" Sullivan suddenly turned to his treasurer and said, "Give me the sack." He opened the sack and took out $400,000 worth of equities. "The man's eye glasses fell off his eyes," Sullivan remembered. "He came around the table and took my hand and said, 'Reverend, we can work together.'" I never forgot that story because it was a lesson in the power of money. With money, you could get things done.

My first experience with community organizing and politics came in college. While attending La Salle , I gravitated to the black Vietnam vets on campus, because I loved their seriousness and maturity. At their urging I organized La Salle 's first black student union and became its first president. At that time, black students made up a very small percentage of La Salle 's population. While there were a ton of different student groups on campus, none represented the views, perspectives, and needs of black students. I wanted the black student union to fill that gap, to advocate for black students and help them get more leadership positions on campus. I wanted to make sure that someone was representing us at the table.

College was a really busy time. I would attend class in the

CB

mornings and work in the afternoons, getting home around eight p.m. to start my homework. But it all paid off – I got a B.A. in English and managed to do it all in three and a half years. After graduation, I taught English in a Philadelphia public school for a year before taking a position with the Urban League as a job developer (I would go on to become director of this program). At the Urban League, I was supposed to find employment for inner-city young adults, many of whom were ex-offenders. This was incredibly hard, because there were more people looking for work than there were jobs. As I looked at the newspaper's help wanted ads each morning, I noticed that the few places that were hiring were all in the suburbs. There was a serious disconnect. This got me thinking.

In order to really help people find work, we needed to find a way to help people get to where the jobs were. I did some research and came up with a proposal for a reverse commute program that involved using shuttle buses to help inner city residents commute to jobs in the suburbs. Coming up with the idea for this program wasn't in my job description, but I knew that if I was really going to help people get jobs, I had to do more than just call employers on their behalf. I had to start thinking about systematic change.

One day I went to a town meeting Senator John Heinz was having at Temple University. I had my reverse commute proposal in hand, and after the meeting, I elbowed my way to the front of the room to tell him my idea. It caught his interest, but unfortunately the idea didn't go anywhere. Still, coming up with this proposal had awakened something in me. It made me see that in order to really help people get jobs, I needed to do more than just help people one-by-one. I had to find ways to change policy at the macro level so that we could create more

22

opportunities for the people who needed them most.

At the same time I was working at the Urban League, I was also getting more and more involved in my neighborhood. Riots in North Philadelphia in the 1960s had started a title wave of disinvestment. Families like mine moved to West Oak Lane because it was a safer neighborhood. But as more black families moved into West Oak Lane, many of the area's white families moved to the suburbs, taking their small businesses and jobs with them. Growing up, I had experienced what a strong vibrant neighborhood looked like and felt like. I knew what it was like to have a neighborhood in which everybody worked and neighbor looked after neighbor. As its demographics and economy changed, however, West Oak Lane no longer felt like the strong community I had grown up in. Crime was up, employment was down, and many storefronts were vacant. Something had to change.

Groups of neighbors started meeting to talk about what we could do to reduce crime and youth vandalism. A lot of people were talking about buying guns for self-defense. I stood up at a meeting and said that was a bad idea. The answer wasn't to buy guns so that people could protect themselves. And the answer wasn't to just increase police patrols, although certainly that was part of it. If we really wanted to reduce crime and make our streets safer, then as citizens we had to work together to build a stronger community. Transformational change doesn't start with government – it starts with citizenship. It starts with us.

Soon after that we formed the Concerned Neighbors Association to tackle problems facing West Oak Lane. The first thing our association did was to go talk to neighborhood kids and find out why they were getting into trouble. They said they just didn't have anything better to do. They were bored. So we came up with plans to keep them busy along more productive lines. We held father-son basketball games, fashion shows, talent contests, holiday parties, and numerous other activities. We even organized tours of La Salle and Temple universities for them. As their community began to invest more in them, these young people began to express a genuine interest in their neighborhood. Soon, they started offering to mow lawns, trim hedges and sweep the streets. In addition to helping motivate our young people, we also spruced up our blocks and began to lobby City Hall for improved public services.

Through my work with the Concerned Neighbors Association, I got to know other leaders throughout the 10th Ward. I developed a particularly strong relationship with Bill Ewing, who was the head of the nearby East Mt. Airy Neighbors Association. When Bill decided he wanted to run for State Senate, he appointed me as his campaign coordinator for the 10th Ward, and I started traveling around to register people to vote. As I did, I was struck by just how little attention elected officials paid to these constituents. Many people had dropped out of the political process because they thought their votes didn't matter. No matter who they voted for, the people who got elected just ignored them.

This line of thinking saddened me. If my neighbors wanted to build a better community – and I knew they did – they had to be active citizens. But what incentive did people have to vote if the people in power ignored them anyway? Many leaders in other neighborhoods shared my concern. Taking a page out of Reverend Sullivan's playbook, we decided to pool our resources to create a group called Concerned Citizens of the 10th Ward. Our goal was to register and educate voters and combat vandalism and vacancy. Even though I was just twenty-one years old at the time, I was elected president. I was just a kid, but people could tell that I was passionate about improving these neighborhoods. They knew they could trust me.

Concerned Citizens of the 10th Ward set out to empower our neighbors. We continued registering voters and conducted a number of meetings educating people about Philadelphia Mayor Frank Rizzo's proposal to change Philadelphia's charter so that he could run for a third term (thankfully, voters across the city resoundingly shot down that idea). We also launched a petition and successfully blocked the opening of an amusement arcade. At this time, amusement arcades were filled with pinball machines and other games, and they could get quite rowdy. In other parts of the city, arcades had brought with them seedy bars, pornography shops, and other undesirable ventures that drew a bad crowd. In blocking that arcade, we put local entrepreneurs on notice that there was now a group of active citizens that was determined to protect this neighborhood's quality of life.

Next I worked with two Republican state legislators to prevent the opening of a bar. And when the West Oak Lane Library burned down, I got it replaced by badgering city officials. Being in my early twenties, I was politically naïve in those days and made some mistakes. For example, I organized a demonstration in front of the burned-out library and neglected to invite or even inform John White, who represented that district in the State Legislature. He telephoned me the next day and told me I was way out of line. But I learned quickly, and the political skills of compromise and negotiation came to me naturally. As I planned events and talked to my neighbors, I was catching the bug. I began to see that problems were really opportunities in disguise. Through hard work and organization, you could improve the lives of everyday people. You could make a difference.

It got to the point where I was working forty hours a week for the Urban League and another forty hours a week for Concerned Citizens. There was a lot on my plate, but I wanted to do it all. After all, I knew there had to be more to life than a college degree, a car and nice clothes. My mom had always told me that we are here to help other people. I wanted to do my part.

As I kept working with Concerned Citizens, the vision that would drive my life – and my years in the State Legislature – came into focus. I wanted to bring West Oak Lane, and other struggling communities like it, back. I wanted to help build strong, safe neighborhoods where people had good jobs, good schools and good communities. That drive would lead me to take on issues that I had never even heard of when I was a kid organizing his neighborhood block by block. Yet in a sense, I can see that everything I have ever done goes back to that desire to make my neighborhood, my city, and my state a land of opportunity for all.

West Oak Lane was a laboratory where I was learning the importance of organizing, bipartisanship, relationships, and money. My work there started to get noticed. In 1979, the *Philadelphia Tribune*, one of the nation's oldest African-American newspapers, named me Philadelphia's "Citizen of the Year." As we approached the 1980s, I began to think about moving from doing things on the ground to trying to affect policy. I had seen the need for systematic policy change in my job at the Urban League, and more and more I saw that need in my neighborhood as well.

One of my heroes is Whitney M. Young Jr., who served as director of the National Urban League before he died in 1971. He always said that one person, working hard, could make a difference. But he cautioned that you've got to do more than make noise. "You can holler, protest, march, picket and demonstrate," he said, "but somebody must be able to sit in on the strategy conferences and plot a course. There must be strategies, researchers, and professionals to carry out the programs." I wanted to get in on those strategy conferences, and I wanted to represent my community's needs in the larger process.

In 1979, all of the 10th Ward, including West Oak Lane, was part of the 203rd District of the Pennsylvania House of Representatives. Even though the district was predominantly African-American, this seat had always been held by a white person, because every two years the Democratic Party's machine managed to split the black vote so that a white candidate could win. Of course, a big reason that the Democratic machine got away with doing this was because a lot of black people had stopped voting, they had lost faith in the political process. As I continued registering people to vote and holding voter education sessions, I realized that I wanted to prove to my neighbors that they could elect someone who would fight for them. And so even though I was only twenty-five years old, I decided to run for State Representative.

If you think that is a presumptuous move for a twenty-five year-old, you're right. I didn't think about my age though. I was young, ambitious and naïve. I saw problems, and I wanted to fix them. People needed jobs, but in neighborhoods like mine there weren't many jobs. By going to the State House, I could create policies that could help change that and improve the quality of life in our community. I could finally show my neighbors that their votes mattered.

In my first run for the Pennsylvania State House in 1980, I had four opponents in the Democratic primary. There were two African-Americans and two whites, one of whom was the incumbent. Historically, many party-backed state legislators from

Philadelphia were just wallpaper at the state capitol in Harrisburg. They sat back and did nothing for their constituents. That had begun to change with the elections of African-Americans like Hardy Williams, Dave Richardson and John White. They were activists and ran as independent Democrats.

I presented myself to voters as a continuation of this movement and an opponent of a Democratic party that was more concerned with perpetuating itself than serving people. In my campaign literature, I used photographs of me with Williams, Richardson, and White. To emphasize my independence, I even used a photo of me with U.S. Sen. John Heinz, the Republican senator whom I talked to about my reverse commute proposal. I already had a reputation for making things happen, and I used newspaper clippings about my recent community activism to show that I could get things done. My campaign slogan was "Now You Have a Reason," and I listed all the reasons people should go to the polls and vote for me. I wasn't making it up. I really had forced changes for the better in my neighborhood. Even though I was just twenty-five, I had a record to run on.

My strategy for the 1980 Democratic primary was to maximize my votes in my own 10th Ward, which was one of two wards in the 203rd District. Although I didn't have any campaign money, I did have relationships. I had a Rolodex of people who I could call upon who were committed to me and shared my vision for reviving this community. My campaign manager, Evangeline Rush, agreed to work for me without compensation on one condition: I had to drive her home every night, no matter what time it was, even though it was a half-hour out of my way. I made that promise, and I kept it. To this day, Vangie is one of my closest friends and most trusted advisors.

In the May primary, I came out of the 10th ward with a huge lead, which was enough to overcome less favorable results in the other ward. I received some 4,200 votes, nearly twice the number of my nearest rival. I easily won the general election in November, and at the age of twenty-six, I became the first African-American to represent Pennsylvanian's 203rd District. When I got elected, I was proud and excited, but more than that, I just wanted to get started.

Before I was even sworn in to office the following January, a woman named Charity Buchanan stormed into my office. She was about four-and-a-half feet tall and spoke English with a Caribbean lilt. She looked me straight in the eye and said, "I voted for you, and now it's time for you to do something! Don't tell me you don't see what's happening. I want this fixed up. I want you to do something about this neighborhood." She described the open-air drug hawkers, the boarded-up buildings, the shuttered homes, the dying trees, and especially Ogontz Plaza, a 30,000 square foot shopping center with empty storefronts, plywood windows, graffiti-scarred walls, and trash-strewn parking lot. "If you don't do something now, I'll never vote for you again!" There was a sting of impatience in her voice.

In my eyes Charity Buchanan is the model of an active citizen. She volunteered in her neighborhood, she voted, and she made sure that those who got elected knew that they would be held accountable. After she came to talk to me, I was more determined than ever to find ways to help create jobs and strengthen these neighborhoods. My constituents couldn't hire a fancy Harrisburg lobbyist to fight for them in the state capitol. By voting for me, they hired me to be their advocate. It was now my job to figure out how to represent them. They had put their trust in me, and I couldn't let them down.

Fixing Broken Windows

When I arrived in the House of Representatives in 1981, I was
twenty-six years old, but I looked even younger. As I sat down
at my desk on the House floor for the first time, someone nearby
whispered, "Who's that kid?" Some people thought I was one
of the teenage pages and would hand me messages to deliver to
other members. The idea that this tall, slim kid from northwest
Philadelphia was their new colleague amused the older, senior
members of the House to no end. They took note of me with
a smile, nodded and then expected me to take my place and do
what I was told.

In those days, freshman legislators were supposed to be
seen and not heard. In the State Legislature, power came with
seniority. The members who served the longest were the ones
who called the shots. Everyone else was supposed to sit back
and follow orders. This line of thinking frustrated me to no end.
Never in my life had I sat back and waited my turn. If I thought
something needed to be done, I just did it. My constituents had
sent me to Harrisburg to fight for them and to find ways to clean
up our communities and create more jobs. I wanted to honor
their trust, but time and time again, my desire to get things
done ran up against the fact that as a new member, I had very
little power or leverage that I could use to pursue my agenda.

CB

During my first term, not only was I a new member, I was a Democrat at a time when the Republicans were in the majority and controlled everything in the House. The Republicans had the attitude that "we are in charge, and you Democrats don't have anything to say." This extreme partisanship was foreign to me, and it was frustrating. I kept thinking to myself: What am I doing here? I had run to become a state representative because I thought that position would give me the opportunity to help my neighborhood. Had I been wrong? I kept hearing Charity Buchanan's voice, urging me to do something, and I felt like I was betraying her. I was so disillusioned that I considered serving out my two-year term and then running for Philadelphia City Council, where I might be able to actually do something. Despite my frustrations, as long as I was in the State House, I was determined to find a way that I could make a difference. One day, I found my opening.

Early in 1982, someone gave me a copy of a confidential memo circulating within the Pennsylvania Department of General Services, the agency which oversaw all of the state's internal operations, including its procurement of goods and services. The document I received stated quite unequivocally that the department was procrastinating in implementing requirements to increase minority participation in state contracts. I was determined to look into this issue, because it struck at the heart of why I came to Harrisburg. The Department of General Services' delays meant that minority-owned companies were losing out on the opportunity to get business that could help them grow and create more jobs. That was totally unacceptable. If we wanted to create more jobs for people in neighborhoods like mine, we had to ensure that minority businesses could compete for business.

32

I looked around for an opportunity to explore this issue, and one soon came up: Walter Baran, the cabinet-level secretary of this department, was scheduled to appear before the House Appropriations Committee to defend his agency's budget request. I wasn't a member of the committee, but nevertheless the chairman, who was a Republican, granted me permission to sit in on the hearing and interrogate Baran. He soon regretted that he did.

When it was my turn to speak, I questioned Baran sharply on why the state was dragging its feet on the contract compliance requirements that were designed to fix inequalities in using minority companies in state contracts. My exchange with Baran became more and more heated, and when I brought up the leaked memo, the attorney for the department accused me of using inside information for political advantage. I responded by saying: "My responsibility as a legislator is to investigate, monitor and be on top of what takes place in all of the departments of this state government. So it is my responsibility to investigate the Department of General Services using any information that is provided to me. Do you have a problem with that?"

Then I looked at the secretary and said, "Mr. Baran, your actions have reduced the Office of Contract Compliance to a non-functioning operation." Baran stared up at the ceiling in utter disbelief. Silence filled the room, but everyone seemed to be asking, "Where does this kid get off talking like that to a member of the governor's cabinet?" The silence stretched on, and finally, the committee chairman told me I was over-stepping my bounds because I was not a committee member. I started to respond, but the chairman abruptly suspended the hearing. I was silenced.

Although my questioning of Walter Baran did not lead to immediate changes, this episode drove home an important point to me: The Appropriations Committee was a heavy-duty, industrial-strength lever that could be used to drive policy outcomes. While I had always known that the Appropriations Committee was the most powerful committee in the House, this was the first time I caught a glimpse of just what that power could do. Each year, every cabinet secretary and every state agency had to go before the Appropriations Committee to present their budget requests. That gave members of the Appropriations Committee a unique opportunity to shape the way that government operated.

The Appropriations Committee's roots stretched back to Pennsylvania's colonial assembly. At one point, Benjamin Franklin headed the committee. He famously complained in 1754: "Both Sides expect more from me than they ought, and blame me sometimes for not doing what I am not able to do." The longer I served on the committee, the more I appreciated Franklin's sentiment. By the time I arrived in Harrisburg (exactly 299 years after the committee was established), the Appropriations Committee was the supreme committee of the House, with its own meeting room and professional staff. After my confrontation with Baran, I knew that if I could get on the Appropriations Committee, I could gain the leverage I needed to get things done. As a member of that committee, I could use the power of money to create new opportunities for everyday citizens and revitalize struggling communities across the state.

During those early days, one of my key mentors was K. Leroy Irvis, a Pittsburgh representative who at this time was the Democratic floor leader. When the Democrats were in the majority in 1977, Irvis had been the first African-America since

Reconstruction to serve as a House speaker in any of the 50 state legislatures. Every time I talked to Irvis about my misgivings and frustrations, he urged me to be patient. Irvis was a truly great man, and I respected his judgment, but I knew that if I was going to stay in the legislature, I had to find a way to get things done. Finally, right before the deadline for me to file the necessary paperwork to seek re-election, I told Irvis I would stay. "But," I added, "If I'm going to stick around and accomplish anything, I need to get on the Appropriations Committee." He said he would see to it that I became a member.

Legislators lead two lives. Half the time you are in Harrisburg, talking to other politicians, attending hearings and policy briefings and, of course, voting on bills. The other half of the time you're home in your district, meeting with constituents and listening to their concerns. Being a neighborhood organizer at heart, I always wanted to be out talking to people and listening to what they had to say. If I was going to represent this community well, I had to know what was on people's minds.

One of the things that was on everyone's mind in the early 1980s was Ogontz Plaza, that 30,000 square foot abandoned shopping center that Charity Buchanan challenged me to clean up before I was even sworn into office. I was obsessed with finding a way to fix up Ogontz Plaza's abandoned storefronts and litter-strewn parking lot. Day after day, I would pace back and forth and stare out my office window at Ogontz Plaza, wondering what to do. I wanted to move as quickly as possible because I worried that my leverage could be snatched away at any time. After all, I didn't know how long I would be in office.

There was never any guarantee that I would get re-elected. And as long as Ogontz Plaza sat mostly vacant, it would be an anchor that weighed down our entire community.

It wasn't always like this. In the 1960s, Ogontz Avenue was a thriving commercial corridor filled with stores. As more black families moved into the neighborhood and more white small business owners moved out, however, things started to change. The number of vacant store fronts increased and the number of jobs decreased. West Oak Lane and other neighborhoods like it ceased to resemble the thriving community I had grown up in. I knew that if West Oak Lane was going to regain its strength – if it was ever going to once again become a community that had good jobs and a vibrant commercial corridor – we had to do something about Ogontz Plaza, because it was central to everything. We had to clean it up and bring it back to life.

The first step in revitalizing Ogontz Plaza was to find out who owned it. By rummaging through some old tax records, I discovered that Ogontz Plaza was owned by a physician named Gabriel Elias, who had a reputation as a slum lord. I telephoned Elias and told him I wanted to discuss some land that he owned in my district. We made an appointment, and I showed up one night at his home in a suburban neighborhood where pristine, expensive houses lined the streets. My intention was to get Elias to fix up the property, which I told him was an eyesore and a liability. When he demurred on the idea, I told him that I was close to Wilson Goode, who was then Philadelphia's managing director (and would soon be elected mayor). Looking him straight in the eye, I made it clear that I would use my clout with City Hall to get the entire building torn down. "If you don't do something, something's going to happen and you won't like it,"

I warned. I was like a dog with a bone, because I knew that the more run down Ogontz Plaza became, the more it would pull down the community surrounding it.

Elias suddenly became very agreeable, and he said he would sell me the property for $150,000. Not knowing anything about real estate development, I initially signed a personal sales agreement for the property. A former colleague at the Urban Coalition lent me $500 for a down payment. I quickly found out that as a state legislator, I could not own and develop this land, because it would be a conflict of interest. I needed an independent entity to take title to the property and oversee its renovation. In short, Ogontz Plaza needed a community development corporation to rebuild it.

At this time, I only had a rough idea of what a community development corporation was. So I had one of my interns, Zenobia Waridi, research what it took to set one up. As a Temple University student and West Oak Lane resident, Zenobia was the perfect person for the job. Based on her research, we created the Ogontz Avenue Revitalization Corporation (OARC) in 1982. Its mission was to create and sustain economic development throughout West Oak Lane. Revitalizing Ogontz Plaza was just the first step.

Over the past thirty years, OARC has used federal, state, city, and private funds to enact our community's vision of a revitalized West Oak Lane. As it has built a track record of success, OARC has become a model for the rest of the city, the state, and the nation. People have come from places as far away as London to see how it transformed a dying neighborhood into a clean, safe, bustling hub of economic activity.

Before any of those successes though, there were years of hard work. When OARC first started, it was run out of my legislative office and managed by people on my legislative payroll. None of my staff had to help out OARC – after all, they didn't get any additional compensation to do it. However, many people on my staff volunteered to help OARC because they cared about West Oak Lane as much as I did. They lived in the neighborhood, and they wanted it to succeed. Today, you couldn't run a nonprofit out of an elected official's office because it is against the rules. At that time, however, it was legal to do so and I thought it was important to nurture OARC and get it on its feet.

I always thought of myself as OARC's number one volunteer. Over the years, because I was in the newspapers a lot, some people got the impression that I ran OARC, but that was never the case. From the beginning, I knew that if OARC was going to succeed, it had to be run by active, everyday citizens. So I set about recruiting board members. I asked Charity Buchanan to be on the board because I wanted to make sure she had a voice in the decisions that were being made. As you might imagine, Charity commanded a lot of respect in our neighborhood, so she could get people excited for the future. Evangeline Rush, my former volunteer campaign manager, was chosen as OARC's first executive director, and Zenobia Waridi was elected chairwoman of the board.

It was also very important that members of the local business community be a part of OARC's board. To that end, I recruited Aurelia Saunders. Aurelia moved to West Oak Lane in the 1970s, and she was one of the first entrepreneurs to open a new business on Ogontz Avenue. When Aurelia opened Fins Seafood Restaurant in 1983, she took a big risk. Even though OARC owned Ogontz Plaza, at that point it didn't have the money it needed to fully restore it yet. Aurelia saw a future in this neighborhood though – she ran a high-quality establishment and her business prospered. I did what I could to help Aurelia and even vouched for her when she applied for a small business loan from the Philadelphia Industrial Development Corporation, the city's economic development corporation, because I knew Aurelia's success was critical to the future of our neighborhood. By proving that a new small business could thrive here, Aurelia's success gave OARC a story it could use to attract other development.

Paul Beale was another key member of OARC's first board. Paul and his wife, Altermese, opened their flower shop on Ogontz Avenue in 1968, and they kept their doors open during good times and bad. Their daughter Paulette runs the store now. Paul was a truly a mentor to me — he taught me what you need to know to run a successful small business. I have always held up Paul Beale's Florist as an example of the type of business that every community needs: It is a home-grown operation run by a group of people who are dedicated to their neighborhood's future.

Once it was formed, I made sure that OARC's board was independent of me. Given that OARC's board members were financially responsible for the organization, they had to be able to run it as they saw fit. I was proud to help start OARC, but I never forgot that its success lay in the community's hands. OARC's board members and I shared a vision for a revitalized West Oak Lane, and we worked hand in hand to make our vision a reality. Although in the beginning none of us knew what we were doing, we learned quickly.

As OARC's number one volunteer, I took it upon myself

to be its chief information gatherer. Through the networking I did as a state legislator, I built a resource bank of experts that I could go to for information and advice. There were academics at La Salle, Temple, and the University of Pennsylvania. I regularly consulted Clifford Jones, who was head of the Pennsylvania Chamber of Commerce and had served as the state chairman of the Republican Party. If people could help OARC, I never cared what their politics were. Cliff put me in touch with Walter D'Alessio, who was a leader in the Philadelphia business community, especially in the field of real estate development. Walt D'Alessio put me in touch with Charlie Pizzi, who was Philadelphia's commerce director. Throughout the 1980s, I was like a sponge, absorbing everything I could learn about economic revitalization from people like Jones, D'Alessio, Pizzi, and many others. Through all these conversations and the readings I did, I was getting my own graduate education in economic development. And all of my knowledge went right back into OARC.

Just like when I was selling tickets, I have never hesitated to ask anyone for help for OARC. After all, the worst thing someone could say was no. Case in point, in October of 1983 I invited Shirley Dennis, the cabinet-level Secretary for Community Affairs, to join with state and local leaders to come see our plans for Ogontz Avenue. A few days later, *The Leader*, our neighborhood newspaper, carried a story headlined, DWIGHT LEADS BLIGHT FIGHT. By bringing together state and local leaders and strategically showcasing our efforts and our plans, we were building excitement. We were beginning to turn the tide.

To really renovate a shopping center, you need money. A lot of money. In 1984, with the help of Republican State Senator

Fixing Broken Windows

Phil Price, we persuaded the state Department of Community Affairs to give us a $900 grant for a feasibility study. It was a tiny sum ($900!), but it was another milestone along the way. Slowly but surely, we were making progress.

Throughout these early years, my thinking was influenced by an article I read in *The Atlantic Monthly* by two social scientists, James Q. Wilson and George L. Kelling. They set forth what they called the Broken Windows Theory, which holds that the way to prevent big problems is to eliminate them while they are small. If you have a building with broken windows and you don't fix them, the theory goes, it leads to more broken windows, then to vandalism, then to a rundown building, then to other rundown buildings, and so on. From there you get neglect and crime. If you fix the few broken windows immediately, you can avoid problems down the road.

With that theory in mind, I started brainstorming with OARC's board about things we could do immediately to change the landscape of our neighborhood. I helped form "Friends of OARC," which consisted of volunteers from the neighborhood who went around picking up trash and painting over graffiti. These volunteers became OARC's foot soldiers in the battle against urban decay. I also reached out to Brandywine Realty to get their help in putting up façades in Ogontz Plaza's windows to make it look like it was occupied. We wanted to give the community an immediate, visual indication that change was coming.

I was always looking for other small things I could do to stop problems before they got out of hand. Sometimes, I had to use a little creativity to get results. I knew right away there were too many nuisance bars in West Oak Lane. It was easier to get a shot of whisky than it was to buy a loaf of bread. I tried to get the

41

state Liquor Control Board (LCB) to shut them down, but I kept running into dead ends. It was obvious to me that the board wasn't exercising proper oversight, especially in African-American areas. They didn't seem to care if there were three or four taverns on the same block. So I introduced a bill that would strip the board of its power to oversee the establishments it licenses and give that power to the Pennsylvania State Police. The bill never passed, but it got the attention of the LCB, which began enforcing the rules and ridding the neighborhood of these bars. This was a turning point for me – I learned that by introducing legislation, I could get people's attention and drive their behavior. That became an important tool in my legislative toolbox.

Of course, to really improve public safety in West Oak Lane, we had to do a lot more than just shut down a bar or two. In the early 1980s, crime was a major problem. It was one of the main reasons why a lot of families kept moving to the suburbs. If we wanted to keep people in the neighborhood, we had to make it safer. I knew the local police district captain, and I persuaded him to establish a police mini-station, which was basically two officers housed in the heart of the community. Local businesses gladly contributed $15 a month to defray the added expenses of the mini-station, which was housed rent-free next to the OARC offices. In a very short period, crime was reduced dramatically. Enhancing public safety was just another piece of the puzzle. Just as you cannot rebuild a neighborhood without commerce, you cannot boost commerce without enhancing public safety. Everything builds on everything else.

People often say that in life, timing is everything. That was certainly the case with OARC. As I was in working to revitalize West Oak Lane, another, much larger economic development project was taking shape in Philadelphia and Harrisburg. In the early 1980s, Philadelphia's leaders knew that the city desperately needed a new convention center. Unfortunately, most of Philadelphia's state representatives, especially those who were African-American, were lukewarm or downright hostile to the $523 million project, because they thought it would take resources away from other parts of the city. As result of other legislators' animosity, Philadelphia's heavy hitters ended up asking me, a thirty-year-old second-term legislator, to lead the effort to obtain state funding and state approval for the new convention center. I quickly said yes because to me, the convention center was a no-brainer. If we did our job right, the city could gain hundreds of millions of dollars in state funding for the project. Just like a revamped Ogontz Plaza would set the stage for new economic growth in West Oak Lane, a new convention center in downtown Philadelphia would be a catalyst for economic growth throughout Center City. In my eyes, it was an opportunity we couldn't pass up.

By 1985, I was fighting for economic development on two fronts. I was working to help West Oak Lane and I was working to line up the funding and support needed to build the convention center. I never saw these two projects as separate. For me, it was never a question of whether you should develop Center City or whether you should develop the neighborhoods. You needed to do both. Indeed, in ways large and small, my work on the convention center ended up directly helping West Oak Lane.

Working on the convention center gave me the opportunity

to continue building relationships with Philadelphia's business leaders. As a result, when I walked into the deep-carpeted Center City office of Hal Pote, the chairman of Fidelity Bank, to try to help OARC get a $1.5 million loan to rebuild Ogontz Plaza, I was not intimidated, even though I had just turned thirty. Hal already knew me and trusted me. We were already on a first name basis. As I laid out my vision for West Oak Lane's revitalization to Hal, I recalled the story of how Leon Sullivan got the bank loan for Progress Plaza back in 1967. When I had finished, I looked at Hal expectantly.

"No problem, Dwight," he said, extending his hand and smiling. I was delighted, but I never thought Hal was doing me a favor. To me this was an opportunity for both of us, a win-win situation. And it was. That loan helped OARC's revitalization efforts shift into high gear, and it was paid back on time.

Through my relationships, over time I was able to help OARC obtain a $500,000 urban development action grant, which was a low-interest loan, from the city of Philadelphia, and $100,000 in financing from the Philadelphia Commercial Development Corporation, which revitalized neighborhoods by making loans to small businesses. As we pulled together the financing, we literally started rebuilding this neighborhood block by block. By 1985 OARC had acquired more properties on Ogontz Avenue. We talked to three developers, but only one–Jim DePetris—was willing to work with us. DePetris was a real estate expert for Rite Aid Corporation, one of the nation's largest drugstore chains. We signed a joint venture agreement with the DePetris Realty Group, Inc., to build a 35,000-square-foot plaza with eighteen stores. It was a good relationship, because DePetris was from Philadelphia. He could bring Rite Aid to the table, and we could give them a lease. The Rite Aid store that we put on Ogontz Avenue was the company's first inner-city outlet. As Ogontz

Plaza took shape, we had a Pennsylvania state liquor store and the Rite Aid as anchors, with local retail in between. We would prove that public-private development projects can work.

The joint venture agreement attracted a lot of attention, because it was almost unheard of– a community development corporation and a private developer working together to build a shopping center. Later, DePetris wanted to do other projects with me elsewhere in Philadelphia, but I declined. My sole focus was West Oak Lane.

Groundbreaking for the $2.3 million Ogontz Plaza project took place in October, 1987. That day was one of the proudest days of my life. One of the symbolic shovels at the groundbreaking was wielded by Charity Buchanan, and for the first time, I thought I was justifying her confidence in me. She and I both had seen that there was a problem with our neighborhood, and through working together, we had found a way to change the course of our neighborhood.

In 1989, the Ogontz Plaza project received the National Council for Urban Development's prestigious National Economic Development Partnership Award. But Ogontz Plaza was just the beginning. As I gained power in Harrisburg, I had access to more resources, and I supported other economic reinvestment projects. Ogontz Plaza snowballed into other economic development projects that collectively came to be called the Northwest Gateway for Jobs and Economic Development. Ogontz Plaza was just one of five centers that sprang forth with banks, groceries and retail outlets. There also are retail developments at the 2300 corridor of West Cheltenham Avenue, the 5300 block of Chew Avenue, 301 West Chelten Avenue, and 1501 North Broad Street. The congregation of financial organizations and groceries is something you don't always see in African-American neighborhoods. It's good for small business owners, and it's good for residents because it gives them a choice when taking out business loans and mortgages.

Government is a service-oriented entity. People want government to work. That is why the military and fire department always have high approval ratings: They provide high quality, direct services that are important to people's lives. Charity Buchanan and active citizens throughout the 203rd District made it clear to me from the beginning that they expected me to get things done. They expected me to make a difference in the life of this neighborhood. They wanted their representative to be a champion for their community. And so I stayed in the mayors' faces, prodded the governors, and used my vote and my leverage and communication skills. Day in and day out, I worked as hard as I could to honor my constituents' faith in me.

ଔ

3

Conventional Wisdom

During my first term in the legislature, Philadelphia's business and civic leaders were trying to get state money to help build a new convention center. Despite the political heft of the convention center's proponents, none of the city's lawmakers, even those in the leadership, wanted to touch this project. In their eyes, it was simply too controversial. Legislators from outside of Philadelphia hated the idea of giving the city millions of dollars in state funding and legislators from Philadelphia itself were either indifferent to the project or viewed it as a rich man's boondoggle. Fighting for the convention center, and introducing the legislation needed to bring it into existence, was a job that nobody from Philadelphia wanted. Nobody, that is, except me.

From the beginning, I looked at the convention center as a no-brainer. Pennsylvania Governor Dick Thornburgh supported it, and he was willing to provide Philadelphia with $185 million in bond issue money under the new Redevelopment Assistance Capital Program to build it. That $185 million would be the largest single state grant in Pennsylvania history and it would help us build a facility the city sorely needed. How could we turn our backs on an opportunity like that?

Although the convention center would be built downtown, miles away from West Oak Lane, I always felt that fighting for the convention center was yet another way to help my neighborhood. After all, not everyone who lived in West Oak Lane could work in West Oak Lane. There had to be jobs in other parts of the city as well. By helping to spark a wave of new development downtown, the convention center would ultimately help create jobs for my own constituents. And so, even though I was only a second-term, thirty-year old legislator, I found myself leading the way on this issue.

Getting state approval and state funding for Philadelphia's convention center was my first big battle in Harrisburg. It would be one of the most challenging and exciting of my career, and it would drive home lessons that I would turn to over and over again in the ensuing decades: There is a give and take to legislative bargaining, compromise is not a dirty word, and a series of one-on-one relationships can trump partisan politics.

Despite the controversy that surrounded it, no one could dispute the fact that Philadelphia needed a new convention center. Conventions were big business, and by the early 1980s, Philadelphia had fallen dangerously behind in the race for the billions of dollars that were being spent in the conference industry. After ranking 12th among American cities in attracting conventions during the 1970s, by the early 1980s, Philadelphia had fallen to 33rd place.

On top of that, Baltimore had opened a new convention center in 1979, Washington opened one in 1983 and Boston had just authorized one that would open in 1987. Our existing facility, known as Philadelphia Convention Hall in West Philadelphia, was outmoded and outdated. If the city was going to attract any major conventions in the future, it needed a new venue to host them.

W. Wilson Goode understood the economics of the situation, and when he became Philadelphia's first black mayor in 1984, one of the first things he did was to get City Council to authorize the new convention center. Yet even though Goode knew we would never be a first-rate city without a first-rate convention center, Pennsylvania's state legislators had no desire to lend the city a hand.

There were many reasons why winning support for the convention center would be anything but easy. First and foremost, there was an historic and pervasive animosity towards Philadelphia among legislators from the suburban and rural areas of Pennsylvania. And I'm not just talking about Republicans. The Democrats from outside Philadelphia were infected as well.

The anti-Philadelphia bias in Harrisburg was part political (Republicans vs. Democrats), part demographic (rural and suburban vs. urban) and, unfortunately, part racial (black vs. white). Moreover, there was an overall impression among lawmakers from other parts of the state that Philadelphia was not able to manage its own affairs and was little more than a drain on the state's resources. This bitterness has followed me throughout my legislative career, and it exists today. In many areas of Pennsylvania, Republican legislative candidates actually publish campaign literature using photographs of their Democratic opponents alongside a photograph of the mayor of Philadelphia. They see it as a kind of guilt by association.

In 1999, Russell E. Eshleman Jr., the *Philadelphia Inquirer's* Harrisburg correspondent, wrote a long article about the anti-Philadelphia bias titled "Why They Hate Us Out There." Eshleman said: "With general unanimity, Philadelphians complain that they get stiffed in Harrisburg. Guess what? Folks everywhere else in Pennsylvania think Mama always liked you best–that the city gets everything it wants." After three decades in Harrisburg, I can say without reservation that more people were antagonistic with me because I was a Philadelphian than because I was an African-American.

But with the convention center, there was another, even bigger, problem than the anti-Philadelphia mindset: There was widespread opposition even among the Philadelphia legislators, especially the African-Americans, based on the idea that this was a project that was going to enrich the city's already rich businessmen at the expense of pressing social needs for poorer citizens.

The perception among African-Americans was that all the jobs involved in building the convention center would go to white people from the Pennsylvania or New Jersey suburbs, and once it was opened the hotels and cultural institutions would not welcome African-American people as visitors. At this time, Philadelphia was seen by many African-Americans as a very racist city. Indeed, there were many black fraternities and sororities in Philadelphia, but these groups never had their national conventions in the city. Why should leaders in the African-American community support a project that was going provide jobs for whites and bring more white people into Philadelphia?

Although I understood and was sensitive to the black community's concerns, I also felt that we had to take a leap of faith. I was very sensitive to the issue of minority participation. (In the early 1980s, most debates on minority participation were focused on increasing opportunities for the black community, which by far was the largest minority in the city. However, as Philadelphia has grown more diverse over the years, talk of minority participation has expanded to include women, Hispanics, Asian-Americans, and other minority groups). I knew we would have to take proactive steps to make sure minorities were included, and I wasn't sure how to do that. But I also sensed that building a new convention center was a once in a lifetime opportunity, and we couldn't let it pass us by.

If we didn't build the convention center, no one would benefit. After we got the convention center authorized, then we could fight for minority participation. President Kennedy was fond of saying that a rising tide can lift all boats. That phrase summed up how I felt about the convention center. I was convinced that the convention center would generate a wave of economic development in Center City that was large enough to benefit everyone.

Before anyone benefitted though, we had to get the funding needed to build the convention center. In April, 1985, Governor Dick Thornburgh said that before he would support the $185 million in state money for the convention center, the entire project would have to be put under public control through the creation of an authority. In addition, the construction contracts would have to be exempt from the city's minority contracting rules. Although we were able to get a clause in the enabling legislation requiring that the authority have an affirmative action program to seek minority participation, there were no hard and fast quotas along the lines that many of the city's African-American leaders were demanding. Therefore, the black legislators, including my friend, mentor and onetime roommate Dave Richardson, remained adamant in their opposition. They wanted the same guarantees for minority participation in the convention center project that the city required of its own vendors. There was no compromising in their eyes. Then, a few weeks later, a bomb was dropped. Literally.

For months, Philadelphia police had been engaged in an armed standoff with MOVE, a black-liberation group that lived communally in a row house on Osage Avenue in west Philadelphia. Neighbors, most of them African-Americans, complained of unsanitary conditions, noisy demonstrations at all hours, gunplay, and other criminal activity. Finally, on May 13, 1985, the police dropped a satchel bomb from a helicopter on the house, and the ensuing explosion ignited a fire that killed eleven people, including five children, and destroyed sixty-five houses.

It was one of the worst tragedies in the history of the city, and it only fueled the perceptions that Philadelphia was out of control and incompetent to manage its own affairs, especially after the initial effort to rebuild the neighborhood was bungled by the city's designated minority contractor. How could Philadelphia be expected to handle millions of dollars from the state's taxpayers? For a while, the convention center looked like mission impossible, even with the support of the Republican governor.

I was determined to push this project through, though. And so to win support for the convention center, I had to become a chess player who was always looking ahead, anticipating my opponents' next move. I knew I had to build support for the convention center from all over the state. So I took time to educate myself about other representatives' priorities. Rep. Sam Morris was a Democrat from Chester County, which had a lot of rural areas. He was very interested in farmland preservation, and there was a proposal before the House to have the state borrow $100 million to help preserve Pennsylvania farmland. I told Morris I would back the proposal. It was not a concession for me to do this, because I genuinely believed in it. I knew how the city was dependent on agriculture. There was a big agriculture school right here in Philadelphia on Ridge Avenue. I also knew that agriculture was Pennsylvania's largest industry. People were often surprised by my knowledge of agriculture issues; they didn't think that a representative from Philadelphia would care that much about farming. But I did.

As part of my efforts to solidify our relationship, I invited Morris to the annual dinner of the Philadelphia Democratic Committee to explain the importance of farmland preservation. When Sam got up to speak, he joked that he'd never seen so many Democrats in one room. After that gathering, Sam and I reached an accord. He understood why Philadelphia's convention center would benefit the entire state, and I understood how farmland preservation would do the same. Jack Stauffer was a Republican state senator from Chester County with whom I formed an alliance along these same lines.

When I started pushing the convention center, I didn't realize how beneficial relationships could be in the legislative process. I built relationships by visiting the home districts of my House colleagues. My philosophy was always that you should treat people the way that you want to be treated. I treated everyone with a sense of respect. I didn't have to give them anything, but I would help them in any way that I could. Some of them were good old boys from blue collar districts. One was a Pittsburgh Democrat named Ron Gamble. Everyone called him "Huck" and philosophically he was very conservative. Other Philadelphians thought he was a racist, but I didn't. I thought he was a man of his word and a man I could trust. We got along. I visited the home of Camille "Bud" George, a Democrat from rural Centre County, and had dinner with him and his wife, Edna. One by one, I sat down with representatives, and I made my case until I got their votes.

Politics is a human capital game, and to play it well you have to know and understand who people are. Everyone is different, and ultimately to get things done you have to have an open mind and a willingness to learn. You have to get people to share your vision, and most importantly you have to ask people for what you want. In getting these people to support me on the convention center, I never simply engaged in a quid pro quo. I built rapport based on the idea that we were all in this together. I just hoped that they could see how we were all interrelated, and how we had to work together. Most of the relationships I secured during the convention center battle were lasting, and they would help me for decades.

One of the greatest hindrances to lining up support for the convention center from around the state was my own Philadelphia delegation's persistent opposition. That sent out a tough message. Other legislators could just say: "Well, some Philadelphians won't even vote for this. Why should we?" But I pressed back with the idea that the convention center was a statewide issue, not just a Philadelphia issue. I emphasized that the entire state would benefit from the convention center because it would raise Pennsylvania's profile. It would draw visitors from across the country and around the world to our state. And it would generate a significant amount of state tax revenue. By investing in the convention center, we were investing in our state's future.

None of this was easy. During the early days of the convention center battle, I was standing at Broad and Chestnut Streets in Center City when a short African-American woman strode up to me, poked her finger in my sternum and said indignantly, "You're Dwight Evans, aren't you? What are you doing supporting this convention center? Don't you know that this is a rich white man's downtown boondoggle that will have no benefit for minorities?"

She told me that her name was Beverly A. Harper, and she was the founder and president of Portfolio Associates Incorporated, a marketing firm. She also headed a "brain trust" that was dedicated to helping minority businesses. She had been the principal proponent of the city's minority contracting program that set numerical goals for city projects, and she was offended that the enabling legislation for the convention center specifically provided that the local ordinance would not govern the new authority. I told her that if she would give me a chance, I would show her why the project was a good thing. We eventually became allies, and she helped me think through finding ways to facilitate minority participation in the convention center.

Even though we were taking active steps to lay the groundwork for minority participation, many in the black community continued to see my support of this project as a betrayal. Black talk radio personalities, like Mary Mason, called me an Uncle Tom. I have a thick skin, but I didn't like that accusation. My black House colleagues thought I was either dumb or had sold out to the white businessmen. The opposition among African-American House members was led by Dave Richardson, who was very angry with me. In their eyes, as long as the enabling legislation did not specifically mandate minority participation and include quotas, it would only benefit Center City business interests and white construction unions. Other convention center opponents chimed in too, raising questions about the cost of the new center.

Now, was the city's white power structure using me? Of course. But I was using them, too. Remember, my advocacy

CR

of the convention center gave me "street cred" with powerful people downtown, like Hal Pote, the CEO at Fidelity Bank (and later a member of the Pennsylvania Convention Center Authority Board), and Fred DiBona, president of the Greater Philadelphia Chamber of Commerce. My role as a convention center advocate also led to relationships with Joe Egan, president of the Philadelphia Industrial Development Corporation, and Bill Hankowsky, the PIDC's project officer who later succeeded Egan. I was able to leverage all of these relationships to help OARC renovate Ogontz Plaza. It was all tied together.

By 1984, the House had passed the $185 million in state capital funds for the project, but the Senate refused to act on the money until the House passed the legislation creating the convention center authority and resolved the minority participation issue. This was tricky. I wasn't mayor or governor, and I couldn't give them the minority participation guarantees that they wanted. But I was working on it. State Senator Hardy Williams, an African-American from Philadelphia, eventually joined me by supporting the convention center in the Senate. I consulted with several law professors, Ralph Smith of the University of Pennsylvania and Carl Singley of Temple University, both African-Americans, about the bill's minority participation provisions. They cautioned me that because of a recent U.S. Supreme Court decision, insisting on hard quotas for minority participation would risk not just the loss of these provisions in state law, it might even endanger the city's minority contracting ordinances.

I believe that my willingness to take this view against numerical quotas, while very unpopular in the black community, helped persuade the Republican legislative leaders–Matt Ryan in the House and Jack Stauffer in the Senate–to support an explicit affirmative action requirement in the state law creating the authority. And I made sure that we complied with all the federal guidelines so we could be sure that language wouldn't get thrown out later.

Everyone had their own position on just what the legislation should say. But I was dealing with a Legislature with 253 distinct personalities. No one was going to get everything they wanted. We all needed the compromise because we all needed this convention center. Again, I told the black caucus that there would be minority participation. "We can't get into a numbers game," I said over and over. "Can you say if it will be 15 percent or 30 percent or 1 percent? No. Can you say there will be participation? Yes, there will be. Absolutely." It was a slow process, but one by one, I established personal bonds with different legislators and recruited their support. It was tremendously helpful that the convention center was backed by Governor Thornburgh. In 1987 his successor, Democrat Robert P. Casey, also came on board.

Nevertheless it was a rocky road for the convention center bill. Twice it was rejected by the House. The first time it got only sixty-eight votes, well short of the 102 votes needed to pass a bill. I was stunned. I thought we had the votes, but it all unraveled as the votes showed up on the electronic board. Some of the suburban Republicans I was counting on saw that there was a lot of opposition coming from Philadelphia itself, and they panicked. As soon as they started switching to no, the Democrats from other parts of the state joined the stampede.

The second time it got ninety votes, closer but still twelve votes shy. Each time the bill went down, a loud, derisive cheer went up in the House from opponents. Before the roll calls, I spoke on the House Floor, saying that the project would create

10,000 permanent jobs and generate $33 million a year in local taxes. But the opponents repeated the accusations that all the contracts were destined to go to white businesses. Some even vowed to physically block the construction of the convention center unless there were minority quotas in the legislation.

Under House rules, you can only vote on a bill three times. Three strikes and you're out. When the convention center bill was brought up for a third time on April 8, 1986, the bill appeared headed for certain defeat. In all likelihood this would have doomed the convention center. I watched in dismay as the electronic roll call blinked. There were more red lights (no's) than green lights. Eight African-American lawmakers from Philadelphia had red lights before their names. "We're cooked," I said to no one in particular.

Then suddenly something totally unexpected happened. The board went blank. The vote was wiped off. Someone had pulled the plug. I was speechless. Nothing like this had ever happened in the House before or since. I glanced up bewildered at the rostrum, where House Speaker K. Leroy Irvis was presiding. He gave me a quick, knowing look and then banged the gavel and called up the next bill. It took me a few moments to realize that Irvis had sabotaged the roll call to save the convention center. Only he could have done it. To this day, the story of Irvis pulling the plug on the convention center vote is legendary among state legislators. It was truly a lesson of the power of leadership positions in the legislative branch.

The next day, the *Philadelphia Daily News* ran an editorial with the headline PA TO PHILA: DROP DEAD! in which it suggested that it was time to reconsider whether to pursue the convention center project. Nevertheless, we decided to continue the fight but we would not bring the convention center to another vote until after the May 20 primary. Once the election was over, a vote for the convention center wouldn't have so many political ramifications.

Despite their persistent opposition, I kept pleading with Dave Richardson and the other black opponents. I said if a Democrat from the suburbs like Sam Morris is willing to risk his seat to support a project in Philadelphia, why can't you vote for it? I pointed out that a major Philadelphia hotel, the Bellevue-Stratford, had just closed, and that most of the people who lost their jobs were African-Americans. But there were a certain number of African-American members from Philadelphia who just weren't going to back us because they were hung up on the minority participation issue. It was a knee-jerk reaction; they thought if the white power structure was for it, they were going to be against it. Case closed.

As we entered the final push in the spring and summer in 1986, I redoubled my efforts to rally up votes from other parts of the state. The most promising area was western Pennsylvania. I knew that public officials and business interests in Allegheny County, which includes Pittsburgh, were pushing for a massive economic development initiative called Strategy 21, which would allow public and private agencies to speak with one voice in requesting state funds. Allegheny County legislators were seeking enabling legislation for Strategy 21, and they wanted it badly. Mayor Goode and I made sure they understood, without our directly saying so, that their bill would not be passed unless there was support for Philadelphia's convention center. It wasn't a direct threat. We didn't need to do that. It was obvious that the two concepts were linked.

Dick Caliguiri, the mayor of Pittsburgh, understood this, and he warned the Allegheny County legislators that continued opposition to the convention center might result in a retaliatory gesture from Philadelphia that would doom Strategy 21. Also, Governor Thornburgh was from Pittsburgh, and he authorized his chief of staff, Rick Stafford, to help shape Strategy 21 and to put all of his energy and talent into securing final passage of the entire package of projects.

We picked up some votes. One of them was my friend Huck Gamble, whose district included the Greater Pittsburgh International Airport. Huck had voted against the convention center in April, but one of the key elements of Strategy 21 was a $400 million expansion of the airport that would require some $100 million in state money. That helped Huck see the light. It wasn't rocket science, and later, he explained his vote this way: "Why make somebody angry when your district is after $100 million?" Indeed!

Next I turned to the so-called upstate Democrats, mostly legislators from the Scranton and Wilkes-Barre areas. Historically, these upstate Democrats are always in a difficult position, because they have strong Republican opposition every two years in their bids for reelection. For this reason, they will seldom vote for a tax increase. Tax votes come from Philadelphia, where most of the members have "safe" seats. But what these upstate Democrats want, more than anything else, are projects–roads, hospitals, state office buildings, and the like. These bolster their re-election chances. They perceived me as someone who could get these passed and funded for them, and I told them that if they wanted these kinds of things, they would have to support me on the convention center. With that, we picked up some more votes.

Irvis and Jim Manderino, the Democratic floor leader, fought hard for the convention center as well. On the Republican side of the aisle, we were helped by the fact that there was intense pressure on the Republican legislators from Governor Thornburgh and business interests, including the Hershey Resort and Entertainment Co. (HERCO), which owned a big Center City hotel.

On June 17, 1986, we brought the convention center up for one final vote. We pulled out all the stops. When we realized that one of our supporters, Rep. Edward A. Wiggins, a Philadelphia Democrat, was absent and attending his son's high school graduation in the city, Irvis and I arranged for the Philadelphia Chamber of Commerce to provide a helicopter to bring him to the Capitol for the roll call. There was virtually no debate on the bill that night because everyone had already had their say. The final vote was 103-93–one more than needed–to pass the bill making the convention center possible. The legislation was sent to Governor Thornburgh, who signed it. Eleven Allegheny County representatives who had previously opposed the measure voted yes. We drew additional support from upstate, and there were even three suburban Philadelphia Republicans who came out in favor of it. But seven African-Americans from Philadelphia remained adamant. Dave Richardson said he would continue his opposition and vowed that the convention center would never be built.

The new law merely said that the convention center authority had to have an affirmative action plan. But a map is not a journey, and I knew that I had to be heavily involved in the implementation of the new law to make sure that language, and the promise of minority participation, became a reality. I spent many sleepless nights worrying that the downtown interests had gotten what they wanted and that I would be left out in the cold. The lawyers told me that as long as there was language permitting minority participation, the convention authority could design its own affirmative action plan.

My first step was to lobby very heavily to have the Pennsylvania Convention Center Authority (PCCA) Board create the post of affirmative action officer. Once I got them to agree to this, I maneuvered to have Ahmeenah Young to be the convention center's director of affirmative action. I knew Ahmeenah because she had done exceedingly well working for Ogontz Avenue Revitalization Corporation. I used my leverage with Mayor Wilson Goode, but his clout had been diminished by the MOVE disaster. The person who really helped me get Ahmeenah named was David Brenner, who was the city commerce director and a member of the convention center board. I wanted to make sure that someone I trusted was there to oversee the implementation of the affirmative action plan. I needed Ahmeenah in there because I needed someone to verify that the affirmative action plan would happen. As I was orchestrating all of this, I kept hearing Ronald Reagan's famous phase "trust, but verify" in my head. I was determined that nothing would fall through the cracks.

Although Ahmeenah's appointment mollified Dave Richardson somewhat, he still never embraced the overall idea of the convention center. All the same, I was immensely proud when

Ahmeenah became president of the Pennsylvania Convention Center Authority in 2008. She was only the second African-American woman to head such an entity in the United States. In my eyes, Ahmeenah's well-deserved success was one more example of how the convention center had expanded opportunities for all.

A few months after the bill was approved, the PCCA imposed a requirement that contractors demonstrate that they have made their "best effort to involve as many women and minorities or firms owned by minorities and women as possible." There was no quota, but the levels of minority and women hired had to reflect "the overall relationship of minorities and women to the general population of the Philadelphia Metropolitan Statistical Area."

But I was thinking beyond the construction to when the convention center would open. How could we make sure minorities got some of the permanent jobs created? I didn't have any answers, but I knew there had to be answers. I called on Beverly Harper, the woman who had berated me on the street for supporting this "rich white man's downtown boondoggle." We met briefly and decided that we needed an entity to implement our vision for minority participation. Then we drew up a list of names to serve on the group. We took our idea to a meeting at the Four Seasons Hotel with Tom Muldoon, of the Philadelphia Convention and Visitors' Bureau; Sam McKeel, the publisher of the *Inquirer*; Bill Giles, the owner of the Philadelphia Phillies, and Bruce Crawley, who was a senior vice president at First Pennsylvania Bank. This meeting set the groundwork for the Minority Advisory Committee (MAC), which was established as an arm of the convention bureau in 1988. Its mission was to aggressively pursue the $3 billion-a-year black convention market.

Beverly did a $7,000 study to examine how best to do this.

She surveyed the literature, talked to travel writers for African-American magazines, and figured out what Philadelphia needed. Out of this research, Beverly came up with eight strategies to make Philadelphia more attractive to minority conventions. When she started the study, Beverly didn't know what the convention industry could do for a city. The study was a learning opportunity for her. Eventually this study not only became a key influence on the MAC, but much of it was also included in the city's convention center law.

I had fought for the convention center out of a conviction that both directly and indirectly, it would create jobs for minorities. At this time, however, only a few African-Americans were working in hotels throughout the city, and there was no pipeline for future employees. There was only one hotel manager who was African-American. We had to find a way to help more minority workers gain a foothold in this industry.

Then, I had an inspired idea. I wanted the Opportunities Industrialization Center–the OIC founded by Leon Sullivan in 1964–to be the pipeline for bringing African-Americans into the hospitality industry. Through providing people with the quality job training they needed, we could make sure that African-Americans could compete for these jobs. But at first Bob Nelson, the president and CEO of the OIC, was resistant. After I pitched my idea to him, Nelson just looked at me with skepticism, saying "Black people don't want to do menial work." I didn't see working in hotels as menial work, though – I saw it as an opportunity to gain a foothold in a growing industry and start climbing the ranks.

Even though Bob Nelson didn't have the same vision as I did, I knew I needed OIC as an entity to train workers. At that time however, OIC didn't do hospitality training. They did workforce training in manufacturing, resume writing, and similar things. But I was convinced that getting OIC to do hospitality job training was the key to creating a pipeline for minority workers. I finally got Nelson on board by getting City Council to direct a percentage of the convention center construction budget for workforce training. I did this through relationships with two City Councilmen, John Street and Lucien Blackwell, who both supported the idea. In fact, the OIC headquarters was in Street's district. Once the funding was earmarked for them, OIC pretty much had no choice but to join our plan. As usual, money drove policy.

And thus the Convention and Visitor's Bureau to some extent became a social entrepreneurship entity. Through the MAC, it was a conduit for minority training, one that is now a national model. Minorities were able to get involved in this growing hospitality industry early. When the Marriott Hotel opened in 1995 on Market Street, Tom Muldoon informed them that either their No. 1 or No. 2 executive needed to be African-American, because that would send an important signal. And now, more than half of the general managers of hotels in Philadelphia are African American. Today, promoting minority staff to manager positions is part of the conversation in Philadelphia's hotels. It is part of the culture.

When we started, Philadelphia was really not focused on hospitality. We wanted to change that. In all we were doing, we were ultimately trying to change the environment of the city to foster more opportunities. As we worked, there was a mood shift. The white business community realized that you could not do this project without including affirmative action. They saw that it was important. Far from being a white man's boondoggle,

CR

the convention center was part of a sea change in the city that opened up more opportunities for minorities. Indeed, in 1992 the *Inquirer* said: "The consensus seems to be that while there have been some failures, the overall record shows that the Pennsylvania Convention Center Authority crafted an affirmative action policy flexible enough to withstand legal challenges, yet strong enough to make a real difference for minority and female workers and entrepreneurs."

The convention center was such a success that ten years after it opened, we decided we needed more space. A $700 million expansion of the convention center, which brought total space to about one million square feet, was completed in 2011. Today, the center is a downtown Philadelphia landmark, and it has had a ripple effect toward improving the city's infrastructure. A 2011 study by the University of Pennsylvania's Fels Institute of Government came to this conclusion:

> Philadelphia today attracts more than 350,000 trade show and convention attendees each year, and 600,000 visitors to gate shows. More people set foot in its downtown convention center than Independence Hall or the Museum of Art. Since the center's opening in 1993, the downtown area has more than doubled its stock of hotel rooms and further stoked a growing hospitality and tourism industry that now provides 10% of Philadelphia's jobs. The multiplier effects of convention business are substantial and easy to see. Most jobs at the center and in the surrounding area are well-matched to the city's employment base and have been filled by Philadelphians. Multiple historic buildings were preserved through conversion, and the ongoing

expansion has bumped up construction employment. Dissenters remain, but their objections are mostly quibbles, and they stand outside a broad consensus. The convention center is a success.

You cannot forget that the convention center would not exist today unless in 1986 we wheeled-and-dealed for votes, offering our support for farmland preservation and airport expansion, pulling the plug on a roll call that would have doomed the convention center, sending a helicopter for a missing legislator, and doing dozens of other things that are not described in civics textbooks. When I think about what it actually takes to get things done in the state legislature, I am reminded of the old saying "Laws are like sausages, it's better not to see them being made."

While the legislative process might make some people queasy, the fact is that the legislative branch was never meant to just be a debating society. It was meant to be a place where reasoned deliberation can lead to decisive action. It was meant to be a place where laws are made that can improve people's lives and create new opportunities for all. That's the bottom line, and you have to be willing to do whatever it takes – within the bounds of propriety and the law – to get the job done.

One of my favorite pictures
with my family, Jean Evans
(my mom), my brothers
Henry, Duane and Gary,
my dad, Henry Sr.
and my sister Linda.

My First Campaign
Announcement for
State Representative
on January 10, 1980
with the late
David P. Richardson,
my good friend
Edgar Howard,
my sister Linda Evans
and others.

(left) Fighting to keep the
West Oak Lane Branch Library open.

(below) Celebrating
the Ogontz Avenue
Groundbreaking with
Councilwoman
Marian Tasco,
Mayor W. Wilson Goode,
Charity Buchanan,
Charlie Pizzi (former
Commerce Dept.
Director) and others.

68

Greeting the late
US Senator
John Heinz and
the late PA State
Rep. Hardy
Williams at a
town meeting
at Temple
University on
January 10, 1980.

Aerial View of Ogontz Triangle
(Circa 1981)

OARC's first official
Board and Mayor W. Wilson Goode.

James S. White, former Managing
Director of the City of Philadelphia.
(Front and Center)

69

Celebrating OARC's first Annual Awards Dinner (photo includes Councilwoman Marian Tasco, Herman Wooden, Zenobia Wardi (OARC's first president), the late Ed Schwartz, Charity Buchanan, Evangeline Rush, Phyliss Benson and others.

Organizing my first Career Day with elementary school principals in my district – Daniel Malone, Leonard Sherman, Richard Salsusky, Beatrice Mickey and Harris Lewin.

Among those celebrating the opening of the NIA Center were the late Dr. Frederick Capshaw, former President of the Community College of Philadelphia (Back Row/Left); David Hornbeck, former Superintendent Philadelphia School District (Back Row/4th from Left); Lynette Brown-Sow, also of the Community College; Dwight Evans; and in front, Phyllis Mitchell, the executive director of the Ogontz Avenue Revitalization Corporation and Phyllis Benson, president of the OARC board.

Charter School Bill Signing with Governor Tom Ridge – June 19, 1997.

Celebrating with the late K. Leroy Irvis (the first African American Speaker of the PA House of Representatives) and his wife Cathy following the hanging of his portrait at the State Capital Gallery.

71

4

The Committee

I never wanted to be speaker of the House. Instead, I wanted to be the chairman of the House Appropriations Committee. To me, the difference between the Speaker and Appropriations Committee's chairman was the difference between a show horse and a work horse. I wasn't the only one who felt this way. More than a hundred years earlier, Matthew Stanley Quay, a powerful Republican political boss, turned down the posts of speaker and majority floor leader and chose instead to be chairman of the Appropriations Committee, which was then called the Ways and Means Committee. Quay knew that that was where the real power resided. It's no accident that the only marble statue inside the Pennsylvania Capitol is of Quay, who served as the Appropriations Committee's chairman in the 1860s.

In many ways, the Appropriations Committee is the House's supreme committee. It is the only House committee whose chairman is elected by the members rather than appointed by the speaker. It is the only House committee whose chairman is part of the chamber's leadership. It has more members (thirty-two) than any other committee, and its meeting room is larger than any other room except the House chamber itself and the two caucus meeting rooms. Moreover, before any bill can come to the floor for a vote, it must go to Appropriations for an estimate of its financial impact (a so-called fiscal note). If you want to get a piece of legislation through the House, you have to go through the Appropriations chairman.

After eight years as a member of the Appropriations Committee, I knew that if I were its chairman, I would have the power I needed to drive policy outcomes. As Chairman of the committee that was in charge of writing the state's budget and allocating state funding, I could use the power of money to help launch new programs and strengthen existing ones. In short, I would have the platform I needed to get people's attention and drive their behavior. The Appropriations Committee's work touched upon all issues I cared about – from job creation to business development to education and more. By managing that committee, I could enact policies that would change Pennsylvanians' lives for the better.

In 1990 I saw my chance. Rep. Max Pievsky, a Philadelphia Democrat who had been the Appropriations chairman for ten years, announced he would not run for another House term. This was fortunate because, in my never-ending impatience, I had considered running against Max for the chairmanship. With Max leaving, there was at least an opening for me, especially since the chairmanship had traditionally gone to a member from Philadelphia. But with anti-Philadelphia resentment was in full bloom, there was a determined movement among Democrats from other parts of the state to elect a leader from somewhere else.

At that time, Philadelphia was in desperate financial straits, and suburban and rural legislators from both parties were reluctant to have the state pay to ease the crisis. Moreover, there was a pervasive feeling that the city was already in a powerful position in the budget-making process. Bob O'Donnell, a Philadelphia Democrat, had just become House Speaker, and over in the Senate, another Philadelphia Democrat, Vince Fumo, was chairman of the Senate Appropriations Committee. Rather than address this anti-Philadelphia sentiment directly, I decided to simply meet with House members one on one and build personal relationships with them. I always thought that I could outwork the unfair bias that faced me, whether it was racism or the fact that I was from Philadelphia. I wanted people to know who I was as an individual, because once they knew me, I was confident that I could win their support. I wasn't going to let racism or regionalism or any other ism stand in my way.

In order to be elected chairman, I needed 55 members to vote for me when the Democrats gathered behind closed doors to pick their parties' leaders in December. I had nine months to get 55 votes. It was time to get to work.

The first order of business was to consolidate my Philadelphia base and get the support of the black caucus. There was still some animosity towards me because of the convention center battle four years earlier. Dave Richardson initially thought he should be Appropriations chairman on the basis of seniority. I had enormous respect for Dave, who was the only elected official who attended my first campaign event in 1980. I would have yielded to him out of respect, but I knew he was too controversial and couldn't win. His dashiki, the huge Malcolm X medallion that hung on his neck, and his aggressive speaking style were polarizing factors that would keep him from getting support outside of Philadelphia. Dave eventually came to agree with me. I also convinced another African-American Philadelphian, Rep. Gordon Linton, that I had the best chance to win. Winning the backing of Dave and Gordon was critical because their districts bordered mine. When you are building support, you always have to start with your base.

CB

My main ally among Philadelphia's white Democratic legislators was Rep. Bill Rieger, a politically savvy, old school street-fighter who had been in the House for four decades. He ran a pizza parlor in Philadelphia and served as a ward leader. Bill was what I call a "retail politician"– meaning that he focused on providing services for his constituents (driver license renewals, cutting red tape with government agencies) rather than affecting public policy.

Bill and I were unlikely allies, but we respected each other. When I came to the House in 1981, he took me under his wing, and we developed a great relationship as co-chairmen of the Philadelphia Democratic House Delegation. He was co-chairman because of his seniority, and I was co-chairman because I was willing to do most of the work. I used to joke that Bill and I had two different styles: He shook the tree, and I picked up the apples. We complemented each other perfectly. Like me, Bill was a fearless advocate for the city. He was the type of guy I wanted to have around. We were both street politicians, and we understood and were unquestionably loyal to each other. Once I started running for Appropriations Chairman, Bill was a huge supporter and ran interference for me with the white members of the Philadelphia delegation. He played a very significant role in my campaign.

But as far as winning the Appropriations chairmanship went, I knew there were only twenty-three votes in the Philadelphia delegation, and I needed at least 55 votes to win. Therefore, I had draw support from other parts of the state, notably western Pennsylvania. This was going to be difficult because all three of my opponents in the race for Appropriations chairman were from this area. Still, I could not afford to get shut out in the west, and so I forged an alliance with H. William DeWeese, who was running for House majority leader. Bill DeWeese was from Greene County, which is in the extreme southwest corner of Pennsylvania. He would go on to become speaker. I also partnered with another up-and-coming legislator, Michael R. Veon, who wanted to become the Democratic whip, which is the assistant floor leader. He was from Beaver County, on the Ohio border. In exchange for their support, I rounded up votes for their own leadership campaigns. We all won in that caucus, and I worked with Bill and Mike for many years in getting legislation through the House.

Through hard work, I even managed to get some support within the Allegheny County caucus, even though two of my opponents for the chairmanship were from that area. Rep. David J. Mayernik, who was from suburban Pittsburgh, backed me for the chairmanship. Dave, like me, was part of a New Generation of House members who had no allegiance to the old ways of doing things in general and the seniority system in particular. Rep. Ron "Huck" Gamble, the Pittsburgh Democrat who had helped me four years earlier by voting for the convention center, wrote me a letter saying he would not support me, but added: "I just want you to know that any votes cast against you will not be cast against Dwight Evans, but rather against Philadelphia."

At this time, there was also a six-way race for the post of Democratic caucus administrator, which is a fairly strategic position because it has the power to assign offices, parking spaces, furniture, and staff. I formed an alliance with one of the candidates, Rep. Fred Belardi, who was from Scranton. In turn, Fred helped me get additional support from Democrats in the Scranton-Wilkes-Barre-Hazleton area. It was a strictly me-for-

CB

you, you-for-me deal. We actually formed a Belardi-Evans ticket.

As I kept working to build my support, I studied each Democratic House member for clues on how I could convince him or her to support me. I learned that Phyllis Mundy had been president of the Wilkes-Barre branch of the League of Women Voters. Based on that, I could tell that she cared about transparency in government, so I won her over by sharing my vision for increased transparency and accountability on the Appropriations Committee. By contrast, my opponents were focused on winning support by promising higher salaries and pensions for legislators. This appealed to a few, but it turned off many others, especially the younger lawmakers.

I knew the race would be close and that every vote would count, so I left no stone unturned. For example, I courted the support of two newly-elected House members who hadn't even been sworn in – Dan A. Surra, from Elk County, an extremely rural area of northern Pennsylvania, and Patricia Carone, from Butler County in the western part of the state. One day around Thanksgiving, I left Philadelphia at 4 a.m. and drove to visit these two. After I sat down with them face to face, both members agreed to back me in the caucus elections. Dan Surra's wife even asked me to stay for dinner, and over meat loaf and mashed potatoes with his family, their ten-year-old son Andy told me I was the first African-American he had ever seen in person. After dinner, I drove back to Harrisburg, making it a round trip of about 650 miles in one day. I told Danny and Pat that the committee would be different with me as chairman, because I would bring our committee's hearings to their districts so its members could listen to what their constituents had to say. "When we come to set up the state budget," I promised, "our members won't just be thinking about Philadelphia and Allegheny County's needs." I kept those promises.

Later some of my House colleagues said they were amazed that I had made such a trip. But in my view, driving hundreds of miles in one day to meet with new legislators was just another form of door-to-door canvassing. I was still doing what I had always done, only now I was taking it to a larger scale.

Now in addition to my race and my region, the fact that I had less seniority than anyone else running was also a strike against me in some people's eyes. But what I lacked in seniority, I made up for in expertise. When I asked members to vote for me, I worked to win them over by sharing with them my knowledge of the budget process, promising to be accountable and accessible, and articulating my vision for creating jobs and improving Pennsylvania's schools. In every meeting I had, I made it clear that I had a vision for the committee. I wanted a committee that would be open to every member, for I had never forgotten my encounter with Wally Baran in 1981 over minority participation in state contracts.

I also made it clear that I wanted the Appropriations Committee to be an independent entity. When Jim Manderino was in power as speaker or majority leader, he effectively controlled the committee. I argued that it should be its own, independent operation, one that had a highly professional and talented staff. Everyone I hired was going to be trained and knowledgeable in his or her subject area.

All in all, it was nine months of hard work. The battle was heated. While my old-school opponents focused on building coalitions within their own areas, I methodically expanded my support to include members from all over Pennsylvania.

CB

I even got support from Rep. Jeff Coy, who was a Democrat from rural Franklin County, which was heavily Republican in voter registration. Jeff, like Dave Mayernik, was from the New Generation. When it came time for Jeff to run for the leadership position of policy chairman a few years later, I supported him.

As I recruited support from other areas of the state, my run for lieutenant governor in 1986 turned out to be a valuable asset. Even though I didn't win, that race helped me develop a statewide profile, which is something that no other candidate for appropriations chairman had. Press all over Pennsylvania knew me. Plus, I had real legislative accomplishments like the convention center, a law tightening the rules for mortgage foreclosures, and the establishment of motivational "boot camps" for nonviolent criminals. Just like when I first ran for the state house, I had a record to run on. And the Democratic caucus was in transition to a whole new way of leadership where seniority was no longer the only thing that mattered.

When I started my campaign, no one thought I had a chance of winning. But the harder I worked, the more members I met with, and the more I laid out my vision of an independent, professional, and well-organized committee, the more support I got. In the end, I just out-hustled my rivals for the chairmanship. I was always the first one in and the last one to leave. I studied the state's budget line by line so that I could show everyone that I knew exactly what I was talking about.

In December, the House Democrats gathered to elect their leaders for the new term. One by one, the members voted for House Speaker, the floor leader and the caucus officials. When we got to the Appropriations chairmanship, they wrote my name on a blackboard along with the other three candidates. As each ballot was opened, another tally mark was set down beside a candidate's name.

Although I was fairly confident that I had lined up enough support, I knew that it was not a sure bet. When the tally began, the suspense built. As more and more ballots were pulled from the box and tallied, however, I quickly outdistanced my three rivals. Within ten minutes there were fifty-five marks after my name. My closest rival, who was from Pittsburgh, had only nineteen votes. There was a burst of applause from all over the caucus room. Several Philadelphians ran out in the hallway pumping their fists in the air. You would have thought I had just been elected president. Even Dave Richardson joined in. Bill Rieger came over and patted me on the back and said, "Good job, kid." As I began to fully realize what had just happened, I was floored by the power that had been entrusted in me and the possibilities that now lay before me. I had just become the first African-American and the youngest person ever to hold this job, which had once been held by Benjamin Franklin. The significance of this moment was not lost on me. I felt like I had just gone to heaven.

The next day, John M. Baer, the Harrisburg correspondent for the *Philadelphia Daily News*, captured the significance of my election with the following words:

> [Evans' victory] comes despite clear anti-Philadelphia feelings in the Legislature, and signals the possibility that Evans and others can put together votes next year for a package of legislation Philadelphia needs to escape from its financial mess, including a controversial local sales tax. It comes despite a hotly contested, four-way race against western Pennsylvania candidates, all of whom had more

C03

---

years of service than Evans; as such, it breaks a tradition of honoring seniority and could mean support for more progressive leadership and ideas. "It sends a message to both new members and older members," said state Sen. Chaka Fattah, D- Philadelphia.

It breaks a racial barrier; former longtime House Speaker K. Leroy Irvis of Pittsburgh was African-American, but Evans is the first Philadelphia African-American ever elected to a legislative leadership post. And yet, several lawmakers said it happened mostly because of Evans' personal style and political acumen. "Dwight ran as Dwight," said Rep. Richard Hayden, D-Philadelphia, "not as a Philadelphian, not as a member of the Black Caucus. He ran on his own merits, and in the end he was the best candidate."

Although there was no textbook on how the chairman of the Appropriations Committee should proceed, I knew right away what I wanted to do. The same afternoon that I was elected, I moved swiftly to consolidate my new power. I met with the top committee staff members, and I told them I expected them to work hard and behave ethically. I didn't want any deadwood on the Appropriations Committee, and I didn't want anyone crossing the line of propriety. I hired a committee controller and told her, "You are the only person who can say no to me. This is the taxpayers' money, and I want you to be certain none of it is wasted." The committee already was staffed by competent professionals, and there may have been anxiety on their parts that of some of the members that I would "clean house" and hire unqualified political supporters. Far from doing this, I raised

82

standards, demanded more work, and added highly qualified analysts. I also created job descriptions, installed an annual performance evaluation system, and even issued a staff handbook setting down my rules and expectations. I was impressed with the work of a committee staff member, Mary Soderberg, and I made her committee executive director. She was the first woman to hold that post, and later she went on to be Pennsylvania's first female budget secretary. When Mary left, I appointed Miriam Fox to succeed her as committee staff director, a role in which she still serves.

I also made it clear that I wanted to appoint the other Democratic members of the committee. I wanted legislators who were going to be diligent about the responsibilities of membership, and I didn't want any lawmakers from a district that would be closely contested in an election. This, I knew, would make them timid about casting difficult votes, especially for new taxes. I didn't get the power to appoint committee members until my second two-year term as chairman, but I knew it was critical to my agenda. I had to have people who would be there for me when I needed them.

I demanded that my committee members toe the line on ethics, and when they didn't, I hammered them. For example, when I learned that one of them had told the CEO of a hospital that the Appropriations Committee would investigate them if they didn't hire his daughter, I chastised him and told him that if he didn't apologize to the hospital executive he would be kicked off the committee.

As Appropriations chairman, I wanted my staff to be my eyes and ears. It was impossible to manage all 203 House members myself, so I assigned staff members to different groups—

CB

Philadelphians, Allegheny Countians, northeastern Democrats, northwestern Democrats, and the black caucus. The job of each of these staff members was to tell me what they were hearing and seeing, what I needed to know. It was part of my management style. My staff was an extension of me, and that's why I wanted them to be professionals. After a few years, my staff people became so responsive that other legislators and lobbyists knew that if they had a budget or policy problem, I was the go-to guy.

When we interviewed for staff positions, we always made it clear that the budget process started in January and went through June, maybe longer. We always asked people, "If the budget isn't finished by July, will you have a problem if you have to cancel your vacation?" We made sure that staff members knew that they had to have cell phones (and later BlackBerries) because they had to be on call 24/7. Some people would say that they didn't want to do that–and so they weren't hired.

I used a bonus system to give my staff incentives. They were always based on performance. If we had an issue with someone, they were given written and verbal warnings. If their issues were not rectified, then these people would not get bonuses. If poor performance persisted, they were let go. But if people were doing well, we would give bonuses after the budget passed. Because of all the recent scandals surrounding the use of legislative staff for political purposes, we had to end this practice. But there was never anything wrong with what we did. Campaign politics were never brought into the Appropriations Committee office, and bonuses were never tied to campaign work. It was very important to me that the Appropriations office was respected and professional. Staff could donate to my campaign, but they were never expected to donate. It was never tied to their jobs.

The Committee

Every year, between Christmas and New Year's, we had a two-day management retreat for staff in my Harrisburg and Philadelphia offices. We reflected on the past year and looked forward to the following one. We would go over subjects like office etiquette, how to use the email system, and how to be politically sensitive. We would hear talks from policy experts. I felt very strongly that it was important for the whole staff to get together at the holidays to celebrate and think about how we could improve. I always wanted to make sure that my offices worked well together so that there was a seamless process through which issues at the local level could be translated into policies in Harrisburg.

After a few years, I instituted budget breakfasts to which I brought in a series of government and academic experts to talk to the committee members and staff. People like Dr. Loren Roth, associate vice chancellor for health services at the University of Pittsburgh, who discussed trends in managed care; Dr. Howard Fuller, director of the Institute for the Transportation of Learning and former superintendent of the Milwaukee School District, who talked about ways to make our schools more effective; and Ted Crone, vice president and economist with the Philadelphia Federal Reserve Bank, who briefed us on the economic framework for the upcoming state budget.

Given how hard my staff worked, I wanted to make sure that our office was a warm and inviting place. Very often, I would walk in to find staffers' children playing in the front room. Indeed, at various points during the summer, my office would turn into Camp Dwight: Staffers' kids would come for the day and build forts using blankets, beach towels and chairs. There were always games and coloring books, and I made sure we had kid-friendly food in the office.

My first big task as Appropriations chairman was the 1991-92 state budget. There was an important backdrop to this: The state had a $470 million deficit, Philadelphia was going broke and headed for bankruptcy, and the Southeastern Pennsylvania Transportation Authority (SEPTA) faced a funding and safety crisis, with no way to repair its crumbling infrastructure and replace aging buses and trains. Early in January 1991, I approached Rep. Matthew J. Ryan, who was the Republican floor leader and a former speaker when the GOP had a majority of the House membership. "Matt," I said, "let's get this budget done." Ryan, whom I came to respect greatly, looked at me in astonishment. "Dwight," he said, smiling indulgently, "That's not how it works." Then his face turned stern. "This is going to be a rough one. Hang on!"

A major obstacle was that although Democrat Robert P. Casey was governor, the Republicans controlled the state Senate. The July 1 budget deadline came and went without any action. State employees were ordered to show up for work, even though they weren't being paid. But they came to the Capitol every lunch hour chanting "Paycheck, paycheck" and carrying signs that said, "Don't Pass the Buck, Pass the Budget!" On July 19, seven weeks into the budget year, we ran a spending plan that included some $2.8 billion in new taxes. Only eighty-five Democrats, well short of the requisite 102 needed to pass the bill, voted for the proposal. There was not a single Republican vote. There was chaos on the floor, and a Democratic member got in a minor fistfight with a Republican.

It was a completely frustrating experience. No one wanted to make a decision, and I couldn't push them to make a deal. It was like herding cats. I didn't like all the back and forth, but I was learning. I was trying to figure out how to get things done, figuring out revenue, expenses, how much money we had and what we could do. I had to keep my eye on the ball. We slowly, painstakingly put together the 102 votes. The Republicans were claiming we could sell off the state-owned liquor stores to private enterprise and use the profits to avoid raising taxes. Privatizing the state's liquor stores was highly controversial and, in my eyes, an unwelcome distraction from the work at hand. I knew I had to separate out the issues of taxes and state store privatization, so I formed all alliance with Rep. Peck Foster, a Republican from rural York County, where there was a lot of opposition to private liquor stores. I truly believed that privatization was a bad idea, and with Foster's support, we were able to defeat the privatization bill and remove that issue from the budget debate.

We were making progress, but then Fred Taylor, a Democrat from Fayette County in western Pennsylvania, balked on the first roll call and voted no. I knew I needed Fred's vote to get the budget passed, so I set out to find out what it would take to move him from "no" to "yes." In the end, I got him to change his vote by inserting a $500,000 appropriation to build a statue of General George C. Marshall in Uniontown, which was part of Fred's district. Marshall, the great World War II general and later secretary of state, was born there. By giving Fred something he wanted, I was able to get something that I wanted. My negotiations with Foster and Taylor drove home the fact that this was how the system worked: If you wanted to get things down, you had to know what made people tick. You have to learn what argument or what policy change would get a member to switch his vote and support your bill.

CԶ

We finally passed the budget on August 4, thirty-six days late, with the help of Matt Ryan and ten other Republicans. Matt Ryan was truly a "Man of the House," and like Leroy Irvis, was honored by having a House office building named after him. The 1991-92 budget totaled $13.9 billion and required $2.8 billion in new revenue, including higher personal income and business taxes and an expansion of the sales tax. I was relieved, but I was also embarrassed. I resolved it would not happen again. This was no way for the trustees of billions of dollars of taxpayers' money to behave.

The following year I introduced a bill that would require each of the four legislative caucuses–House Democrats, House Republicans, Senate Democrats, Senate Republicans–to introduce a proposed state budget by the third week of May for the fiscal year that ended June 30. My intention was to keep the Legislature on target for approving a budget on time. I took a lot of heat from my own party on this. In fact, Fumo called me a "nitwit" for disrupting normal budget negotiations. This bill was passed by the House, but it died in the Senate. Nevertheless, I got my message across about avoiding embarrassments like the 1991 fiasco, and for the next three years we passed the budget on time. In fact, in 1993 we approved thirty days before the end of the fiscal year–a rare achievement in legislative history.

Soon after he took office in 1993, President Bill Clinton announced a plan to "reinvent government," declaring: "Our goal is to make the entire federal government less expensive and more efficient, and to change the culture of our national bureaucracy away from complacency and entitlement toward initiative and empowerment." I wanted to do the same thing at the state level. A reinvention of state government was exactly what we needed. I decided to focus on the Appropriation Committee's ability to evaluate the performance of the programs and agencies it was funding. I urged other House committee chairmen to look at their oversight responsibilities. In an interview with *Governing Magazine*, I said: "My experience has been that we're really not clear on why we do what we do. If something's not working, we shouldn't be fearful of saying that."

The magic number was always 102 votes, the barest House majority. My question was always, "What will it take to get your vote?" Sometimes it was a no-brainer.

One year Casey sent over a budget that eliminated two state-supported institutions–the Scotland School for Veterans' Children, which was in Jeff Coy's district, and the Scranton School for Deaf and Hard-of-Hearing Children, which was in Fred Belardi's district. I knew neither of them was going to vote for a budget that eliminated these schools, because they provided jobs for their constituents. So I put the money for them back in the budget, and they came through for me in the final roll call.

The first time I saw Jerry Maguire, I laughed out load. In the movie *Jerry Maguire*, Tom Cruise says to Cuba Gooding Jr., "Help me help you." That's the message I conveyed when I was rounding up votes. Sometimes it was a new highway; sometimes it was a ticket to a baseball game; sometimes it was an appointment to a House committee. And sometimes you had to get their attention by taking something away–a staff member, an office, a new state building. The message was: If you don't do what I think you ought to do, I'm going to make your life unpleasant. The Appropriations Committee was a full-service operation. My position was: If what you want is legal and reasonable, I'll do it. If it involved money we didn't have, I would move it to the next year's budget. As chairman, I didn't have total control, and so I used these tools. I made deals, but it was never for my personal benefit. It was to achieve my vision of strengthening communities and creating opportunities for all Pennsylvanians.

Sometimes I could just appeal to my colleagues by saying, "Look, you were elected to do a job here, and you're not doing it." And for a lot of these legislators, this was a great job and they didn't want to mess it up. During budget votes, I'd remind them that if they didn't pass the budget on time, they weren't going to get paid. I'd go up and down the aisle a lot during roll calls. I'd tell them, "You can give me your vote now, or you can give me it later. We either do this now, or we don't get paid." Legislators only got paid once a month, so this was a potent argument. "Tell that to your wife and kids. Tell them you didn't get paid because your didn't get the job done."

Moving and influencing politicians is not easy. I was like the conductor of an orchestra. I would spend hours with people trying to figure out what it would take to get them on board, "You tell me everything you need, and I will look at it and just go down the list." You need to be a student of the process. If you want to succeed, you couldn't just be a student of the process... you had to be at the top of the class.

Much of my power grew out of the fact that I knew more about the budget than anyone else. I would spend a lot of time studying the budget and meeting with cabinet officers and the budget secretary. I knew every line item in the budget, which in those days was a three-inch book of numbers, and I knew what the analysts did. Governor Ed Rendell once said that I understood the state budget better than anyone he had ever met. I studied it inside and out. I knew the importance of knowing the numbers and how numbers drove outcomes. In other words, the key to driving behavior of others was my knowledge of the budget. It was a blend of politics and policy. I was obsessed with remembering everything about everyone. I knew the personalities behind the budget requests. A politician really can make a difference and really can do good. But you can also be overwhelmed by the process and lose focus. I never lost focus. I was very clear about both my mission and my passion. In later years, when I dove deeply into issues like education and public safety, the budget was my policy implementation tool.

The Pennsylvania House of Representatives is always closely divided between the two parties, and I knew that I needed Republican votes to achieve my vision. On many issues, it was easier to deal with the Republicans from the Philadelphia suburbs than it was with the Democrats from western Pennsylvania. I almost always had a cadre of between ten and fifteen Republicans whose votes I could count on. They were not only from the suburbs, but also from rural areas. I had always championed agricultural issues like farmland preservation, and I had their respect. I needed these GOP votes to counter-balance some of the Democrats from the west who would not do the right thing and didn't know how to act. They were caught up in the anti-Philadelphia nonsense.

ဿ

If the governor was a Democrat, as was the case for the first four years with Bob Casey, I would help carry his initiatives as well as mine. I worked well with Republican Tom Ridge, who was governor from 1995 until he became head of Homeland Security in 2001.

Democrat Ed Rendell was governor from 2003 to 2011. I already had a close relationship with him from his days as mayor of Philadelphia. When Rendell was governor and Democrats had a majority in the House, there was not much that I could not get done. Rendell would not sign off on a budget unless I agreed to it, and that gave me power. Even when the Republicans controlled the House, I could advance my agenda, because the Republicans realized that I could lobby Rendell to veto their budget if they did not include some of my priorities. For example, I was able to secure $30 million for the Fresh Food Finance Initiative when I was in the minority because I had leverage.

Operationally, the budget-making process worked this way: There were six of us–the chairman and minority chairman of the House Appropriations Committee, the chairman and minority chairman of the Senate Appropriations Committee, and the majority floor leaders of both legislative chambers. We sat around a table and decided the budget. Staff members sat along the walls and were consulted from time to time. There were a lot of expenses that had to be paid up front: debt service, pensions, school subsidies, prison costs, and huge Medicaid bills owed to hospitals and nursing homes. We would pay all these bills and then account for the governor's new programs. If the governor was a Democrat, I would help carry his initiatives, too.

Sometimes I would get into a conflict with the governor

about his agenda and I would remind him, "We have to do things for the legislature, because that is how we will get the votes to pass the budget."

Once that was done, we would determine what was left for the Legislature and apportion that amount among the four caucuses. I only focused on the members in my caucus and what they wanted. I always had a wish list from my members. I always got a laugh from the other leaders when I'd say, "My people have needs." Some examples: We gave $300,000 for a program providing housing and support services for recovering alcoholics. There was $6 million for summer jobs for students. Many of these involved specific projects in members' districts, such as repairing a much-beloved library or strengthening a key job training program.

I respected my members, and I wanted them to be able to get funding for initiatives that were important to their districts. If someone brought me a bad project, however, I would try subtly to discourage them from seeking funding for it. I didn't tell members no outright, but I did try to steer them in the right direction by giving them advice on how to rank their priorities. Of course, when it came to allocating money, you could never satisfy people's appetites. I had to do the best I could, because that was how we got votes for the budget. This was how the system worked – if you wanted to get the budget passed, you had to give people a personal stake in it. Politics is not for the faint-hearted. If you want to get something done, you've got to know how to move people from no to yes.

As the years went by, some members looked at me as an ATM machine. Since I was Appropriations chairman, they were convinced that I held all the purse strings and I had the power to give them everything they wanted. Of course, that wasn't true. Yes, I had a lot of power in shaping the budget, but I couldn't make money grow on trees. I was constrained by the economy, the revenue projections, and the political landscape at the time. No one seemed to understand the pressure I was under.

When they got frustrated, some of my colleagues would point fingers and say there was too much money going to my district. Looking back, I think they were jealous of me. They didn't understand that a big reason why I was able to fund and launch important projects was because I had a very clear vision of what I wanted to accomplish. I knew I wanted to help build strong communities by tackling issues including education, public safety, and job growth. I was constantly out talking to people to figure out who had the best ideas and which projects could really make a difference. I did my homework so that when it came time to do the budget, I knew exactly what money I wanted to put where.

I was sensitive to members' criticisms though. I didn't want to rile people up, and so I didn't seek a lot of media exposure at check presentations and ribbon cuttings. I knew that the competition would seize upon that as evidence that I only helped my own neighborhood. In reality, I wasn't only focused on helping my district – I was focused on helping the whole state. I visited as many districts as I could, and I never hesitated to go off the beaten track. Indeed, in some of these places I went I was the first black man people had ever seen. I kept track of everyone that I helped, but some members were always more interested in what I got and what other members had gotten than in what I had done for them. They didn't understand that it took a lot of work and thought to get the results that I got in my own neighborhood.

The Committee

I was constantly on the lookout for opportunities to help West Oak Lane. One year I got some money to enable the Philadelphia Orchestra to go to China. To show their gratitude, the leaders of the orchestra offered to let me go along with them. I didn't care about going to China, however. What I cared about was bringing the orchestra to West Oak Lane. So, I told the orchestra's leaders that if they wanted to thank me, they could offer a free concert every year at Martin Luther King High School. And with that started a great tradition that lasted until I left the chairmanship in 2011. There's no way to measure how valuable these concerts have been for kids in terms of getting them interested in music. The concerts were standing-room-only every year.

I believe my request for free concerts was totally justifiable because it was not for my personal gain, it was for my district's and the city's benefit. Being transactional is not a bad thing if you are being transactional to be transformational. I believe that being exposed to music can be a transforming experience for a child, and I am proud that through supporting a worthwhile project for the Philadelphia Orchestra, I could bring that opportunity to West Oak Lane.

Another time, Joe Neubauer, the chairman of ARAMARK – a huge company that provides food and other services to schools, hospitals, and other institutions – approached me in his capacity as chairman of the Orchestra. He asked for state funds to help build what is now the Kimmel Center. I saw that the project was worthwhile, so I agreed to help. Down the line, as a result of our relationship, Neubauer gave $50,000 in personal funds and $50,000 in Neubauer Family Foundation funds for Simons Recreation Center in my district. Some people looked at this as quid pro quo. It wasn't. I had a twenty-five-year relationship with Joe, and out of that relationship, he learned about and was motivated to invest in my community. This is just another example of how relationships lead to results.

Much has been made of my use of campaign contributions to gain and hold power. Because I had a safe seat (and let me emphasize that my seat was safe because I delivered for my constituents), I didn't need a lot of money to conduct my primary and general election campaigns every two years. Although my vote for a bill authorizing a state takeover of the Philadelphia schools resulted in a tough primary in 1998, most of the time I was unopposed. But as my power grew in the Legislature, I was able to raise huge amounts of money for campaign funds, which I in turn gave to other House members who had more difficulty winning reelection. Sometimes I gave more than $1 million to my fellow Democratic members in a single cycle. My primary goal here was to keep Democrats in control of the House so that I could advance my agenda about jobs and economic development.

In later years the media focused on these campaign contributions as the sole reason I stayed on as chairman. But it was never about that. My power came from the relationships I had with my fellow members, and campaign contributions were just one of many tools I used. Sometimes I would get support from a Republican legislator by promising that I would not donate to his or her Democratic opponent. And a lot of this money was coming from Republican business interests in Philadelphia, with whom I had been building relationships since my support for the convention center.

It's hard to know how much a legislator is influenced by a contribution, but money is like oxygen to a political campaign. When I ran for the first time in 1980, with four opponents, I spent only about $15,000. Today, even an average House campaign costs $100,000, and highly competitive races cost much more.

I know that the role of money in elections is a problem today, but I was focused on getting things done, and these campaign contributions were just another way to do that. As money has an important role in politics, I'm going to use it. I may not agree with the baseball rules that allow batters to bunt and steal bases, but as long as those rules stay in place, players owe it to their teams to take advantage and steal bases where they can.

When Democrats would call and ask me for campaign money, I would usually give it to them, because I wanted to keep our majority so I could realize my legislative goals. But it was never quid pro quo. Case in point, in 2010, some of the legislators that I gave money to joined other Democrats in voting me out of the chairmanship just a few weeks after the election.

Pennsylvania Democrats faced a brutal election year in 2010, it was a brutal election year for Pennsylvania Democrats. We lost the majority in the House and a Republican governor was elected. When the House Democrats held our leadership elections a few weeks later, a majority of the caucus members voted to have someone else chair the Appropriations Committee. After 20 years, my tenure had come to an end.

While I had known it would be a tough vote, I was still surprised by the results. After all, I had had tough leadership votes before, and I had always come out on top. When I lost, many people assumed that I would be devastated because I loved serving as chairman. It was a disappointment, but to be honest,

୧

I was ready to move on. Being chairman of the Appropriations Committee was an all-consuming, 24/7 endeavor. No one, not even me, could keep up that level of intensity forever.

When you are responsible for approving or disapproving specific initiatives in specific legislative districts, you can make a lot of enemies over two decades. And I did. The move to oust me as chairman was led by western Pennsylvania lawmakers, but some Philadelphians joined in. Their rap on me, in general, was that I was sending too much money to my own district at the expense of other areas of the city. I obviously felt this was grossly untrue but regardless of the facts, nothing would change these members' minds. Even in the midst of this hostile environment, the vote against me was only 45-43.

In addition to having made some enemies by saying no to certain things, my candidacy for chairman was also hurt by the fact that many of my strongest allies were no longer in the House. Most of the House's New Generation, people like Dave Mayernik and Jeff Coy–had left. Additionally, in the 2010 primary election, I had supported Bill DeWeese's Democratic opponent. (I did this because just before the primary, there were rumors swirling around the Capitol that DeWeese was going to be indicted on corruption charges.) By this time, I had reached the end of my rope tolerating the low esteem accorded the Legislature by the public. I kept hearing my grandmother's lecture about right and wrong. I went to DeWeese and said, "Bill, I don't know if you did anything wrong, but if you did you ought to resign." He didn't deny doing anything wrong, and he didn't quit, and so I supported his primary opponent in 2010. DeWeese won anyway, and the following November he worked hard to unseat me as chairman.

When I lost my chairmanship, the people from the

neighborhood thought I had lost my seat, and I had to reassure them that I would still represent them. They didn't always understand the difference between the two jobs. I'm sure people thought I was devastated, but it was hard to keep up that hustle to do that job well. I didn't want to leave, but once the vote was over, I felt relieved. I was ready to move on.

After the chairmanship vote, I sent a letter to all House Democratic members:

> I want to thank you for the privilege of serving on the House Appropriations Committee for 28 years, the last 20 as chairman.
>
> It was an honor to represent you and your constituents at the budget table during that time. I was particularly delighted to visit your legislative districts so I could learn about the people, places and programs that make Pennsylvania thrive.
>
> In good economic times and bad, we forged ahead regardless of the political situation. In doing so, we never lost sight of our Democratic values: to protect our most vulnerable citizens: children, seniors, veterans and the disabled. We fought for working families, union rights, funding for education and healthcare for all. We didn't win every battle, but we raised the dialogue and the expectations.
>
> I am proud of the changes we made in the spring budget process. A simple numbers crunching exercise is now a more strategic process that analyzes programs, performance and spending.

Dozens of members served on the committee through the years and went on to chair standing committees. I thank those members and all who served on the committee for their hours of hard work in trying to make sense of a complex and often confusing process. What's more, with your help, we were able to open the budget process to citizens from around the state.

The end of my term as chairman of the Appropriations Committee marked the end of an era. As I packed up my office and said goodbye to my staff, I felt a tremendous sense of pride. I had set out to make the Appropriations Committee a highly professional, highly effective organization, and I had done that. I had helped to get funding for countless projects that bolstered Pennsylvania's economy and expanded opportunities. The two decades I spent pouring my life into that committee was time well spent.

5

The Power of Money

It was very late one night in May 2007, but I didn't hesitate to call Lisa Renee, my office manager. I didn't have to tell her who was calling, so I just started right into it: "I need a million dollars."

"We don't have it," she said without hesitation.

"Find it and call me back. Deb Kula's constituents have no access to water."

I had just left the Brownfield Community Center in Fayette County, which is in southwestern Pennsylvania, more than 200 miles from Philadelphia and one of the poorest areas in all of Pennsylvania. Rep. Deborah Kula, a freshman Democrat, had told me there were people in her district who had no water.

I was at the tail end of a week-long swing through western Pennsylvania that was part of my mission to get out of Harrisburg regularly and see how state money was being spent and where it was needed. Deb Kula had asked me to listen to her constituents for five minutes, so I agreed. I was an hour late, and she was very nervous because she feared I wouldn't show up. She had told me earlier that no legislative leader had ever visited her district.

I was weary and baggy-eyed as I shook hands with local officials and community leaders. When I got to a guy named Charlie King, he said, "Don't shake my hand unless you're going to help us." I shook his hand, pulled up a chair, turned it backwards, sat down and told him I was not there to give him lip service and really wanted to hear what he had to say. When he started talking, I was shocked.

King said many people in Old Tyrone Township did not have running water in their homes and had to haul their water from wells in big plastic tubs. Many of these wells were polluted and were starting to run dry. In one instance, a house burned to the ground because the fire department didn't have the water needed to put it out. Charlie had conducted an informal water survey, and he said that one well's water looked like urine.

"People shouldn't have to live like this," he said. I told him I couldn't agree more. I couldn't believe that in the twenty-first century, in the United States of America, there were people who didn't have a decent water supply.

Others spoke up. They were literally begging for water. They looked sad. They had struggled for so long and they had very low expectations. I hated the idea that these people were not getting a fair shot. I thought: People have lost faith in the political process. They think the system is too complicated now for them to be able to exercise their rights. There was no question that this water situation was one that the private market would not address on its own. The economic incentive just wasn't there. Government needed to help. As I walked out of that meeting, I thought, Damn it, we have to help these people. That's when I called Lisa Renee at home.

Finding the $1 million was difficult, because the end of the fiscal year was little more than a month away. Nevertheless, less than a week after the meeting in the Brownfield Community Center we came up with the money by shaving funds from other programs, including some initiatives in Philadelphia. When we put it together, we pulled Deb Kula out of a caucus meeting in the tiled hallway of the Capitol and told her. She was in total disbelief. Her knees literally went out from under her and we had to catch her. She said Fayette County had never gotten $1 million for anything. And now she could go home and tell people that their long-delayed water project was getting kick-started.

The first important point I want to make with this story is this was not a political exercise. I did not have to go to Fayette County to get Deborah Kula's support for my Appropriations chairmanship. I already had her support. I went to her county because I felt like it was an important part of being Appropriations chairman. It was important for me to go out and see first-hand where the money was needed.

The other important point was that the project bringing water to the homes of people in Old Tyrone Township was a WAM, which unfortunately is an acronym for "Walking Around Money." These are earmarks, whose proper name is Pennsylvania Legislative Initiative Grants, that provide funds for specific projects. There was a second earmark program, RACP, which refers to the Redevelopment Assistance Capital Program (it doesn't work very well as an acronym). Earmarks have been roundly defamed in Washington and most state capitals as wasteful spending on legislators' pet projects. But I believe that most of the WAMs and RACPs that went through my committee were for worthy projects. Moreover, earmarks were an important part of the overall process of getting things done in the legislature.

There's nothing new about earmarks. They're older than Pennsylvania. In fact, it began in 1751 when Benjamin Franklin sought legislative approval for an appropriation of 2,000 pounds for the construction of Pennsylvania Hospital, which was the first hospital in America. It was opposed by rural lawmakers, and so Franklin, ever the wheeler-dealer, proposed a compromise: If the backers of the hospital project could raise 2,000 pounds from private sources (which would indicate there was widespread public support for the institution), then the Assembly would match the donations with a 2,000-pound appropriation. Hospital supporters came up with the money, and so did the legislators. It was the first matching fund project in Pennsylvania. The hospital opened in Philadelphia in 1756. Franklin was delighted. "I do not remember any of my political maneuvers, the success of which gave me at the time more pleasure," he reflected.

Both WAMs and RACPs began under a Republican governor, Dick Thornburgh, who worked closely with Jim Manderino, the powerful Democrat who was the House majority leader. WAMs started out very modestly, but they grew every year. The legislature's four caucuses would apportion the money evenly among themselves and then each would decide how to distribute it to individual members. The money went for things like local parks, sewer and water projects, and aid to volunteer fire departments. Handling this through the four caucuses actually saved money, because we avoided the kind of free-wheeling pork barrel spending that goes on in the United States Congress. Much was made about the secrecy of WAMs, but in most cases the individual members issued press releases and otherwise trumpeted their role in getting the popular projects approved.

The RACP was invented by Rick Stafford, who was Thornburgh's secretary of legislative affairs, as a means to finance Philadelphia's convention center in 1986. They differ from WAMs in several important aspects: Applicants for the money must raise a matching amount of money and undergo an extensive review by budget officials. The state borrows the money through bond issues, and so these expenditures aren't included as part of the state operating budget. The rationale for borrowing the money is that the projects carry long-term benefits.

There were a lot of RACP projects under Democratic Governor Bob Casey (1987-1995), Republican Governor Tom Ridge (1995-2001) and Republican Mark S. Schweiker (2001-2003), but they really surged under Democrat Ed Rendell (2003-2010), who approved nearly $2 billion in RACPs for sports stadiums, museums, and industrial expansions. Most of these projects were intended to stimulate the economy by providing jobs.

During my twenty years as Appropriations chairman, from 1990 to 2010, the city of Philadelphia was literally transformed. We built the convention center, the Barnes Museum and the Kimmel Center, all with the help of RACPs. The city, the nation's fifth largest with a population of 1.5 million, made the transition from an industrial center to an economy that was based on culture, information, and service. Drawn by the convention center, Independence Hall and the Liberty Bell, some two million people visited Philadelphia in 2011. RACPs and WAMs funded city projects like the Arthur Ashe Tennis Center, the Asian art initiative, and youth hockey. The city is one of the largest research and health education centers in the U.S. Led by the Philadelphia Museum of Art, the Pennsylvania Academy of the Fine Arts, the new Barnes Museum, the Franklin Institute, and the Pennsylvania Historical Society, there are dozens of museums and galleries dedicated to the visual arts, science and history that benefitted from these grants. I'm proud to have had a role in all of this.

A study by the Greater Philadelphia Cultural Alliance released in 2012 concluded that the city's arts and cultural organizations have had a huge impact in stimulating economic activity, including job creation, in the Philadelphia region. It is said that these institutions, most of them bolstered by RACPs and WAMs, are responsible for injecting some $3.3 billion annually into the area's economy.

I worked closely with Governor Tom Ridge, a Republican, to provide $320 million in state subsidies that helped build new stadiums for the Philadelphia Phillies, the city's Major League Baseball team, and the Philadelphia Eagles of the National Football League. This was a long, tough battle because the anti-Philadelphia sentiment was intense. It was offset somewhat by the fact that the same money was earmarked to build new stadiums for the Pittsburgh Pirates and the Pittsburgh Steelers. Even so, we had trouble rounding up the votes. What finally sealed the deal was that we inserted a provision that if the new stadiums didn't provide the state with $300 million a year in new tax revenues, the team owners would have to make up the difference. Thankfully, this has never been necessary because the stadiums have been a success.

Shortly after I became chairman I was approached in the hallway of the Capitol by Bill Strickland, whom I would soon learn was a remarkable man who had developed a unique job training operation in Pittsburgh called the Manchester-Bidwell Training Center. Strickland, an African-American, had grown up in an impoverished Pittsburgh neighborhood and began working with poor people while a student at the University of Pittsburgh in the 1960s. He established the Manchester Craftsmen's Guild, which was designed to introduce adolescents to the arts, and then he took over the Bidwell Training Center, which provided vocational training to young adults. This became the Manchester-Bidwell Training Center in Pittsburgh.

As I listened to Strickland describe his program, what appealed to me most was that he was taking entrepreneurial ideas and applying them to social problems. Manchester-Bidwell was a successful model of combining government, private enterprise and philanthropy to a job creation program. It developed programs in partnership with companies in need of highly skilled workers. Nearly 80 percent of adults who enrolled there completed their vocational training, and 86 percent got good jobs. What distressed me about our conversation was that a legislator had promised Strickland state funding, but now he believed they were reneging. I didn't like the way he was being treated, and so I invited him to my office. We immediately connected, and within a few weeks I had gotten a $50,000 WAM into the budget. This would become a regular annual budget item.

As I got to know Strickland, I realized he was something of a genius. Indeed, in 1998 he won a MacArthur "Genius" Award. I developed a long-term relationship with him, and he really influenced my thinking on workforce development. My experiences with Bill Strickland expanded my vision and interest in the critical matter of getting people jobs. Strickland also became a strong resource and political base for me in western Pennsylvania. In addition to Manchester-Bidwell, I studied a program in Detroit called "Focus: HOPE" and another in Cleveland called "CAMP"– the Cleveland Advanced Manufacturing Program. One thing I noted about all three was that they tried to stay ahead of the curve by anticipating where new types of jobs would be needed and avoiding jobs for which there was decreasing demand. The question right in front of me was this: How could we train under-employed people in the Philadelphia area to take manufacturing jobs that were leaving the region because of the lack of qualified workers? I read everything I could on the subject and learned about factories that had been converted to job training facilities in Germany and Japan. Then I saw the answer right in my own neighborhood. For many years, the Penn Emblem factory at Stenton Avenue and Haines Street had employed about two hundred local residents who made uniform emblems. Then it closed in 1994. I didn't like seeing an abandoned factory in my district. "How much money will it take to have OARC buy this factory?" I asked my staff. The answer was $350,000. We arranged the financing secured with a WAM, and OARC bought the building. Once we got site control–we had a big celebration when they turned over the keys–we went to work. No one had ever done anything like this before.

In 1996 we created the Philadelphia Area Accelerated Manufacturing Education, "PhAME," whose mission it was to offer specialized skills training in the field of computer-based precision machining and manufacturing technology. The initial funding was $7 million, and it was a combination of federal, state, and city funds plus loans and grants from private foundations. The biggest chunk, some $3.5 million, was an RACP. The initial participants in this unique program were OARC, the Community College of Philadelphia, and Lehigh University.

We formed an alliance with Crown Cork & Seal, which manufactured packaging products in northeast Philadelphia. The company was looking for machinists but could not find enough qualified applicants, and they agreed to help fund PhAME. We made a substantial investment, around $25,000, in each of the students. They went to school six days a week for fourteen weeks. Part of the money went to support the trainees' families while they were in school. I believed, and I still believe, that such an investment in training will eventually result in new tax revenue and less spending on social programs.

The program drew substantial praise from local employers, but we had to drop it in 2002 because it was felt it was too expensive. I think this penny-wise-pound-foolish attitude has changed, and that the climate today would support it.

Although I was constantly accused of funneling all the money into my own district, any time I was asked for funds for a worthy project, I seldom hesitated, no matter where it was. As long as it was in Pennsylvania. In 2003, Rep. Jake Wheatley of Pittsburgh came to me with a request for money for a Sheltered Bonding Program to help businesses owned by minorities and women compete for state contracts. This, of course, is a topic near and dear to me. The program was the brainchild of a young man named Marc Little, who was himself an African-American contractor who saw that many of these businesses had trouble competing because they did not have enough capital to get the required bonding. I got a $1 million WAM for Wheatley to get this program under way because I believed in the idea. Once the state money was there, the foundations started contributing to the program. And it worked out. The agency has had great success in providing increased opportunities for minorities and women, especially in the building trades industry.

After a few terms as Appropriations chairman, I tired of the staged protests that were held at the Capitol and usually organized by lobby groups. I decided that I needed to get out of

Harrisburg and into other areas of Pennsylvania. I would meet with local officials, community groups, service clubs, ministers, small businessmen, PTA presidents, and anyone with a cross to bear or an axe to grind. When you see the problems from ground level, you see how important these WAMs and RACPs are to real people.

When I went into budget negotiations, the information that I gathered on these trips helped me make decisions about where to direct RACPs and WAMs. When I was at the negotiating table, I would think about the people that I had met on my travels. To a legislator, every project that is important to their constituents is important to them. But I had to prioritize things—we couldn't fund everything. And in many cases, these kinds of trips helped me do that. WAMs were not done in isolation. They were done in the context of things that I had seen. It is one thing to talk to a legislator about a project, but it is another thing to be with the people who are involved with a project and to see first hand what a certain project means to a community.

The term "pet project" is a very subjective one. One man's pork is another man's prime beef. On one occasion I was making a speech in Ellwood City, which is a tiny borough with some 8,000 residents thirty miles northwest of Pittsburgh. When I was finished talking, I went for a walk by myself and after several blocks came upon the Ellwood City Library. I went in and introduced myself to two ladies who were the librarian and assistant librarian. They told me that they were desperately in need of more space and needed $500,000 to relocate to a new building. I looked around. There were boxes full of books piled to the ceiling. I remembered how important the neighborhood library had been when I was growing up, and I said to myself,

Here I am and something needs to be done and I am going to get it done. I almost never promised people money on the spot, but I promised them. There were tears in their eyes. When I went back and my staff asked me where I went, I told them: "I was at the library. They need $500,000."

A few months later, the library had WAM for $575,000 to help them relocate. Even though I had a big role in financing projects like this outside Philadelphia, my position was always that the member should get the credit because he or she represented that community. In this case of Ellwood City, the grant was announced by Rep. Jaret Gibbons, the local House member.

As a result of public anger over a legislative pay raise voted in 2005, dozens of incumbent legislators were defeated in 2006, and the following year I decided it was important to hit the road and build relationships with the new members and hear from their constituents. I had just hired Johnna Pro, who had been a reporter for *The Pittsburgh Post-Gazette* covering state government during the Ridge administration. Later she worked for Lieutenant Governor Catherine Baker Knoll. I liked Johnna because she was a straight shooter. I did not always agree with her, but I appreciated that she would give me the opinion of someone outside the Harrisburg culture. Johnna was very cynical about state government when she started working for me, but by the time she left in 2011 she saw how hard we were working and that we could really make a difference.

Johnna accompanied me on the 2007 trip, which began in Erie. Our plane landed about 5 p.m., and ninety minutes later we had a meet-and-greet at a local club. About forty people showed up. The next morning we met with the Erie County commissioners, and then Johnna started driving south. Over the next two-and-a-half days, we visited seventeen counties, met with a dozen legislators and heard from local people. We looked at a soccer field in Mercer County, a youth center in Westmoreland County, and a tech school in Washington County. One town wanted a new fence for a PONY League baseball field, another wanted to renovate an old movie theater, and another wanted a new senior center. It was always important to me that everyday citizens, and not only local politicians, attended these events. I went on these trips because I wanted to hear what people on the ground had to say.

WAMS have been demonized. Some people abused them, but most of them didn't. I know what I did, and it's well documented. If a member came to me and asked for money, I didn't just give him a check. There was a process: The representative had to put in an application to the Department of Community and Economic Development, justify the project, and get it approved. RACPs were different, mainly because there had to be matching funds from another source. Someone disparaged RACPs as "WAMs on steroids." But that's not right, because these projects had to have community support and community funding.

But without RACPs and WAMs there would be no outcomes. No new library in Ellwood City, no water for the people of Old Tyrone Township, no job training program in Pittsburgh, no free concerts in Philadelphia. These types of projects lift people up and enrich their lives. They don't start with money. They start with a vision. Vision must precede money.

Some legislators wouldn't focus on what they were getting; they would just focus on what others were getting. You could never satisfy their appetites. They would say, "Look how much is going to Philadelphia." But I worked very hard to show people that I was fair. And I didn't let my personal feelings get involved—I would give money to legislators that I didn't like, because I knew that the money was a good project for their constituents. And, of course, there was always the implicit, and sometimes explicit, threat from legislators: If you don't give me money for this project, I won't support you for Appropriations chairman next time. It was a situation that would even have vexed Ben Franklin.

The truth is that WAMs and RACPS, far from being an extravagant waste of taxpayers' money, have provided critical investments in public structures such as libraries, courthouses, medical facilities, educational institutions, urban business corridors and even sports stadiums and arenas. Dozens of communities statewide have reaped the benefits of these programs. These targeted government investments have made a real difference in people's lives.

Moreover, WAMs have provided funds for important social programs. Back in 1993, Robert J. Reinstein, dean of the Temple Law School, wrote a letter to *The Philadelphia Inquirer* that was headlined, "Temple Dean lauds WAMs:"

"Some questions that have been raised about Pennsylvania Legislative Initiative grants (WAMs) prompt this letter.

"Reductions in state support to higher education threatened two of Temple Law School's most important programs. Temple-LEAP is a 19-year-old program in which our students teach about law and civics in area high schools and organize a citywide mock trial competition.

"This program has been very successful in motivating high

school students to continue their education and to consider law as a career. And, for the last 40 years, students in the Temple Legal Aid Office have been providing free legal representation to poor people in Philadelphia. Without this assistance, many people with valid legal claims would be unrepresented in court.

"In response to the state's cutbacks, Rep. Dwight Evans, who chairs the House Appropriations Committee, arranged for Temple Law School to receive Legislative Initiative Grants in support of Temple-LEAP and Legal Aid. Through his efforts, and with additional support from federal granting agencies and private sources, we have maintained these two programs, which provide invaluable educational experiences for our students and important public services for many people in Philadelphia."

The current debate between austerity and investment is foolish. It's thinking small. You have to make investments to spur development. You do not need a lot of public money, but you do need some. If Pennsylvania is to be the business-friendly destination that the governor and my colleagues claim they desire, we need to do more, not less, to entice the private sector to invest its dollars and manpower in the commonwealth. The convention center spurred extensive private investment in hotels, restaurants, and condominiums. This is still going on today. Public and private projects are interconnected.

Not only did WAMs and RACPs provide money for worthy projects, they were an important tool that all legislative leaders and all governors used to get things done. They were the grease that got blockbuster bills through. Remember it was a WAM for a statue of George Marshall that finally broke the budget deadlock of 1991. In a state as closely politically divided between Republicans and Democrats as Pennsylvania, legislative paralysis is always a threat. Rounding up the 102 votes needed to pass a bill in the House is never easy, and sometimes getting a major educational reform through depends on widening a four-mile stretch of highway in somebody's district. Is the trade-off worth it? Absolutely.

∛

ᘓ

6

The Gang of Five

Much of my time as Appropriations chairman was spent dealing with the problems afflicting my city. Twice during these twenty years I sought a more direct role by running for mayor. I was unsuccessful, and after each loss I doubled my efforts to effect change from my legislative seat of power.

When I assumed the chairmanship in 1990, the city was on the brink of chaos because it was about to run out of money. We had delayed taking any action in Harrisburg until after the 1991 mayoral election because we feared there would be huge upstate voter rebellion against anything that could be perceived as a state bailout of the city.

The historic anti-Philadelphia animus in Harrisburg had been bracketed and given a coefficient because of the police bombing of the MOVE headquarters in 1985. Wilson Goode, who was in the last year of his second term, had lost the support of Philadelphia's business community and had zero credibility in Harrisburg. He was seen by many as part of the problem rather than part of the solution. As a result, when I became Appropriations chairman, many in the city feared a catastrophic collapse of city services–no garbage collection, no police in the streets, no firefighters.

The city's political structure was paralyzed, and I knew any

117

solution was going to have to come from Harrisburg. I knew we had to impose change in every area of urban policy. While Democrats controlled the state House, Republicans held the upper hand in the Senate. The GOP Senate leaders were adamant: The city was incapable of managing itself, and they would not support any bailout that did not include at least a temporary state takeover of the management of the city's financial affairs.

The city's finances were so shaky that credit agencies downgraded its bond rating to junk level, and it was unable to get a short-term loan to temporarily balance its budget.

I believed that part of any solution had to be granting the city the power to solve its own problems by imposing new or increased taxes; any new or increased city taxes had to be authorized by the state legislature.

But this change was not going to happen as long as Philadelphia was perceived as unable to handle its own affairs. There were warring political factions within the city, notably those loyal to Senator Vince Fumo and others aligned with Congressman William H. Gray; I tried to serve as a buffer.

In the end we came up with the Pennsylvania Intergovernmental Cooperation Authority, which was a state board to oversee Philadelphia's finances. It issues bonds on the city's behalf and regularly monitors its finances. The PICA was charged with "restoring the financial stability" in Philadelphia. The city was empowered to pass a 1 percent sales tax.

There was factional warfare over PICA that had racial overtones, and I was in the middle. On one side were Jonathan Saidel, the city controller; Bob O'Donnell, the House speaker; and Vince Fumo, the Senate Democratic Appropriations chair. They were all white. They and the city's leading bankers, also white, favored a state control board like one established in New York City, a board of appointed officials that could overrule the city's elected officials with respect to expenditures, labor contracts, and major purchases. On the other side were Mayor Goode, Congressman Gray, and a number of African-American officials who favored increased state and federal aid and giving the city new taxing power and the ability to finance its deficits without strong state controls.

In the middle was John Street, City Council's Appropriations chair, and his black and white allies on Council, who had passed a resolution calling for the establishment of a cooperation authority that could borrow funds and provide them to the city in exchange for the power to approve the city's five-year financial plans. State oversight under this model was restricted to determining whether the financial plans were balanced; the board would have no power to overrule specific decisions of the city. And the terms of the agreement between the board and the City had to be approved by City Council, hence the key word "cooperation" with the state, not "control" by the state.

But because all of these approaches required state legislation, I was in a key position to influence which approach was followed. Even though I had reservations about all of the approaches, I tried to keep my eye on the ball. I knew that something needed to be done. I could see how all these developments would affect West Oak Lane and the convention center. I knew that as the city goes, so goes West Oak Lane. It was all interconnected. I knew major changes were needed, but I didn't think that outsiders could micro-manage the city's finances.

In the end, I favored the Street approach, not just because I felt that the cooperation model preserved the authority of local elected officials to make specific budgetary decisions, but also because lawyers I respected told me that the New York control board model would have violated the Pennsylvania Constitution; I was sure the state would not help the city without some ability to insure it balanced its budgets over the long run. PICA turned out not just to work in Philadelphia, but it also was copied in other cities that faced fiscal distress.

What erased my misgivings about the overall proposal was its requirement that the city submit five-year budget projections. This afforded ultimate transparency. The proposal also provided that each of the four legislative caucuses would name a member of the PICA board. I felt this gave elected officials oversight over PICA.

As it turned out, the five-year projection requirement proved critical for Mayor Ed Rendell, who succeeded Goode in 1992, because the forecast showed a looming billion dollar deficit. The dark shadow enabled Rendell to wring major contract concessions from the city's powerful public employee unions.

The entire battle over the city's finances left a bad taste in my mouth because of all the partisanship, Democratic-Republican bickering. I came away from this with the knowledge that if I was going to achieve anything in Harrisburg, I would need help from Republicans. In later years I would be "accused" of bipartisanship by some fellow Democrats. I plead guilty.

For the first six years of my chairmanship, I worked hard on city issues and succeeded on many occasions, but I was continually frustrated by the extreme political partisanship, especially within the Philadelphia delegation. Finally, in 1997, I reached out to the Republicans, and eventually I put together a bipartisan coalition that would come to be known as "The Gang of Five."

The Gang consisted of three white Republicans–Reps. John Perzel, John Taylor and George Kenney–and two African-American Democrats–Rep. Anthony Williams and me.

The roots of the Gang of Five go back to a trip I made to New York City in 1996. For several years, I had been distressed by the level of crime in Philadelphia and its impact on our economic development. I have always seen police as economic development officers. You cannot rebuild a neighborhood or a city without commerce— and you cannot boost commerce without enhancing public safety. The two are inseparable.

I met with William J. Bratton, who as police commissioner under Mayor Rudolph Giuliani, had instituted policies based on the Broken Windows Theory, which I had been espousing since my first efforts to improve my West Oak Lane neighborhood (see Chapter 2). Bratton believed that if petty crime is not reduced, all crime will increase. Moreover, he advocated a police force that ethnically reflected the population, and he developed a positive police relationship with law-abiding residents. He also put in place a system of computerized crime-mapping. As a result of Bratton's policies, New York's crime rate fell sharply while during the same period Philadelphia's was rising.

You have to understand that this was a daring move. Rendell was a highly regarded mayor, and there was a general feeling that when it came to any city problem, he knew best. So here I was not only challenging that assumption, but also going to talk with a man who had worked for a Republican mayor (Giuliani), who was held in low esteem by the black community. Who was

CR

I to challenge Rendell's articulation about how to run a police department?

But I came away from my meeting with Bratton convinced that we needed his policies in Philadelphia. Rep. Anthony Williams agreed with me. Then the three House Republicans– Reps. Perzel, Taylor and Kenney—went to talk to Bratton, and they were similarly persuaded. The Gang of Five was formed, and we scheduled a series of high-profile town meetings on crime. We brought Bratton in as one of the first speakers. Rendell was bitter, saying the Gang of Five was engaging in an unwarranted meddling in city business.

As African-Americans, Williams and I took a lot of heat from the black community because the city's police commissioner at this time was Richard Neal, who was an African-American. Here we were bringing in the white guy, an outsider, to criticize our black police commissioner.

But our support was critical because it was an against-the-grain move, similar to President Nixon going to China or President Clinton passing welfare reform. No Democratic president could have opened China, because it would have been viewed as selling out to the Communists. No Republican president could change the welfare system, because it would have been viewed as being cruel to poor people. And in 1997, Republicans by themselves weren't going to shake up the Philadelphia Police Department because it would have been viewed as a racist.

But under Richard Neal, the Philadelphia police were so focused on serious crimes that they were ignoring the neighborhood crimes–vandalism, burglaries, auto theft. I thought this was totally wrong and at odds with the successful Bratton model. I wrote an op-ed page piece in the *Philadelphia*

The Gang of Five

Daily News in which I said "the Philadelphia Police Department is still unfocused, untrained and under-equipped."

After the hearings, I urged Rendell to hire Bratton as a consultant. He was resistant at first, but he finally saw the light. This led to forcing Neal to resign as police commissioner and replacing him with John F. Timoney, who had been Bratton's top deputy in New York. Not only had Timoney put Bratton's reforms into place, he was in charge of training, hiring, and promotions, and he oversaw the merger of the transit and housing police into NYPD. By the time he left in 2001, Timoney had brought the city crime rate down.

In the months that followed, Perzel told any who asked that the ouster of a black police commissioner and his replacement by a white could not have been achieved without the support of African-American legislators. The race of the police commissioner didn't matter to me at all. I just wanted to improve the Police Department.

But the Gang of Five was just beginning. We passed twenty-three pieces of legislation that targeted nuisance and quality-of-life crimes. For example, Timoney told us that there wasn't enough space in city jails to keep arrested prostitutes off the street, and they had to be released. We proposed that the city be allowed to set up tent cities during the summer months to accommodate prostitutes and other nonviolent offenders. Other bills dealt with graffiti, smash-and-grab cars, break-ins, and speedier court disposition for minor offenses. Rendell endorsed them all. Most of these bills passed the House, but unfortunately died in the Republican-controlled Senate.

When I ran unsuccessfully for mayor in the 1999 Democratic primary, I made crime the No. 1 issue. I did this because the people had told me over and over that the most pressing issue they faced was lawlessness. Several polls backed me up. I pledged that if I was elected, I would take my oath of office in front of the federal courthouse, and then walk into the court and sue the big gun manufacturers for damages because of the high cost of dealing with violent crime.

It was a bruising, complicated, five-way election in which three of the candidates–City Council President John Street, former City Housing Chief John White Jr., and I–were African Americans. An early poll had me in second place, but then Rendell threw his support to Street, the eventual winner. Rendell at this time was enormously popular, widely called "America's Mayor," because he had balanced the city budget and had rung up five straight years of budget surpluses. My support plummeted, and I ended up with about 5 percent of the vote.

Although I lost the primary, after Street was elected mayor he held a press conference with me and announced that he was going to sue the gun manufacturers. The courts eventually rejected the lawsuit, but we did raise public consciousness on an issue that needed to be addressed.

When I ran for mayor in 2007, I pledged to fly down to Miami and persuade Timoney, who was police chief down there, to return to Philadelphia, because I didn't like what was going on with the Police Department. The commissioner at that time, Sylvester M. Johnson, was an African-American, and once again I was heavily criticized. However, after Michael Nutter won the Democratic primary and then was elected mayor, he reached outside the department and replaced Johnson with Charles H.

Ramsey, who had served as chief of the metropolitan police in Washington, DC. Ramsey increased the number of cops on the beat, moving them out of patrol cars and on to foot and bicycle patrols, and he installed surveillance cameras at dangerous intersections. The crime rates dropped.

So despite losing in the 1999 and 2007 mayoral primaries, I managed to effect positive change through my candidacy.

Next the Gang of Five also waded into the longstanding controversy over the funding of Philadelphia Schools in 1998. When Superintendent of Schools David Hornbeck threatened to close the schools unless there was more state funding from Harrisburg, we pushed a proposal for a state takeover of the school system. We got tremendous opposition from the Philadelphia Federation of Teachers, and the head of the Philadelphia NAACP said I should be removed from office. I was condemned by the *Philadelphia Tribune*, an African-American newspaper, while I was praised by *The Wall Street Journal,* which has very conservative editorial views. My support for this legislation led to the Philadelphia Federation of Teachers backing my opponent in the next primary election (see Chapter 7).

Despite all the opposition, I managed to maneuver the bill through the House; it was approved by the Senate and signed by Ridge. The new law provided for the takeover of the Philadelphia School District by the School Reform Commission. My position on this was simple: If this is what it takes to keep the schools open and provide educations for the children of Philadelphia, so be it.

One of the biggest issues to come before the House was riverboat gambling in 1998, which would have raised millions of dollars for Philadelphia public schools. This was a statewide issue, and so the Gang of Five was brought into play.

We knew that Pennsylvania residents were dropping about $1 billion a year in the casinos of Atlantic City, which was sixty miles from Philadelphia. Wouldn't it be better if they dropped that money in Philadelphia? Plus the thousands of tourists who come to the city every year to see the Liberty Bell and other historic attractions also would try their luck aboard one of the boats cruising the Delaware River. It seemed like a no-brainer. If Pennsylvanians were going to lose the money anyway, why not lose it here?

The proposal would have allowed riverboat gambling on any navigable waters in Pennsylvania, and therefore it was popular not just in Philadelphia, but in the cities of Pittsburgh and Erie and even in southeastern suburban counties like Bucks.

Most of the opposition came from conservative legislators, both Democrats and Republicans, who opposed gambling on principle and who warned that the floating casinos would generate crime and tarnish the image of the City of Brotherly Love. Moreover, the lawmakers came from districts that would not qualify for the casinos.

I was in the middle of running for mayor, and my support for riverboat gambling was vehemently opposed by the African-American clergymen, who were a potent political force in Philadelphia and who threw their support to my opponents.

Rendell and I had been trying to get this measure passed for several years, but Governor Ridge said the only way he would sign such a bill was if it was approved by Pennsylvania voters in a non-binding referendum. This was an unusual strategy, and it was designed to give the GOP cover from the anti-gambling interests.

The Gang of Five

The timing was critical because we wanted to get the question on the May 18 primary ballot. It was an unusual referendum, because while proposed constitutional amendments often appear on the statewide ballot, no one could recall the last time a non-binding policy question like this was put before the voters.

We brought it up for a vote in February, and on the first roll call it fell ten votes short of passage. But I wasn't worried. We knew the "nay" votes had come from rural lawmakers, who were responding to the anti-gambling beliefs of many of their constituents. We argued that the casinos would create good jobs. I got a printout of statistics showing what the bill would mean to the whole state. I went to each of the recalcitrant members with the printout; I highlighted the specific benefits to their districts with a yellow felt pen. Printouts like this are always a valuable tool. People can see exactly how a bill is going to impact their districts in terms of jobs and revenues. Though he kept his active role behind the scenes, Perzel helped me round up some Republican votes.

On the next vote, the bill passed with six votes to spare. But it was all for naught, because a month later the Republican-controlled Senate shot the proposal down on the grounds that it was unconstitutional. Vince Fumo, the powerful Democratic Senate leader, did not want the question on the ballot, because he believed it would somehow generate votes for my mayoral campaign because I was associated with the referendum. In other words, Fumo allowed mayoral politics to trump what was best for his city.

Despite the defeat of the gambling referendum, the Gang of Five continued to fight on issues of vital interest to the city of Philadelphia. It was a unique, unprecedented use of bipartisanship

൫

toward good ends. Suddenly longstanding goals that had been thwarted by partisanship were sailing through the House.

John Baer wrote a long article about us for the *Philadelphia Daily News*, and in it he quoted Stephen MacNett, who was the chief counsel to the Senate Republicans and had been around the legislature for nearly four decades. "The city has been historically represented by several camps and factions," MacNett said. "To see a bridging between black members and white members, R's and D's, shows a new collective willingness in Harrisburg to deal with urban issues, something that since the late 1970s, maybe before, the Legislature has been reluctant to confront."

All members of the Gang took heat from others in their own party. Many House Democrats accused Tony Williams and me of betraying the party. Republicans said Perzel was power hungry, and they said I was just furthering my own aspirations to become mayor. But we were functional where before there had been dysfunction. The criticism of the Gang was muted after we chalked up success after success. And in my view, none was more important than charter schools (see Chapter 7).

I ran for mayor again in the 2007 Democratic primary. Since Philadelphia is a heavily Democratic city, the democratic candidate almost always wins in a walk, so the primary is the race that matters. I finished fifth with only about 8 percent of the votes. For a few days I was stunned and disappointed. But then I got back on my feet and went to work in Harrisburg. I told everyone that 92 percent of the Democrats in Philadelphia wanted me back at the state Capitol. And then I got down to work.

CR

The task was daunting. Governor Rendell submitted a budget that included seven tax increases. Republicans in the House and the Senate vowed there was no way they would vote for new taxes. I had a one-vote Democratic majority to work with in the House, and some of those Democrats were taking a no-new-taxes stance. Nevertheless, we managed to pass the budget.

One thing working in our favor was that between February (when Rendell unveiled his budget) and June, state tax collections picked up and the need for new revenue was lessened. Then we put together a plan to raise tolls on the Pennsylvania Turnpike and use the additional money to fund mass transit projects. This gave us a budget that did not require any new taxes.

When the smoke cleared in mid-July, the *Inquirer* ran an editorial headlined "DWIGHT EVANS: CITY'S FRIEND:"

> Pennsylvania finally has a budget, two weeks late. Nobody worked harder to get it done than State Rep. Dwight Evans (D., Phila.).
>
> Evans is chairman of the House Appropriations Committee, a job he approaches with energy, urgency and optimism.
>
> He needed those qualities to help achieve the reasonable $27.2 billion budget state legislators aimed to wrap up last night.
>
> Working with a one-vote majority in the House, Evans had been handed a proposed budget by Gov. Rendell containing seven tax increases. Even some House Democrats vowed to vote against any tax increase, as did the Republican-controlled Senate.

CR

Cast as the man in the middle, Evans navigated his way to a spending plan that doesn't increase taxes but still achieves many of Rendell's solid priorities. They included a $300 million dedicated fund for mass transit, and a big spending increase for pre-kindergarten programs.

"The budget contained a 5.5-percent increase for education (with a desperately needed additional $77 million for the Philadelphia School District). It aims to bolster the quality of day care for children of low-income families, and to expand home and community services to thousands of elderly and disabled people. All are among Evans' priorities.

He drew a line in the sand over transit funding, saying there would be no budget deal without it. The day after Evans took this stand, he admitted to feeling a little bewildered and disappointed that he had received 'no calls' of support from elected officials in the Philadelphia region. He had a right.

Throughout the sometimes unproductive negotiations with Senate Republican leaders, Evans kept his sense of humor. At one point, he described his give-and-take with reluctant Senate negotiators this way: 'I gave you food; now you owe me a hostage.'

It was impressive work by a lawmaker who was coming off of a tremendously disappointing performance in the Philadelphia Democratic mayoral primary.

That was a crushing result for a man who had long dreamed of leading his city. But Evans wasted not a second pouting or stewing. He went straight back to work in Harrisburg, and did his job masterfully.

Democrats had told him get back to Harrisburg and work on his agenda there. Today Pennsylvania residents are the better for it."

CB

Throwing a Hail Mary for Education

Education was very important in my family. My mom and dad always told us that we had to go to school and we had to work hard. I went to Philadelphia public schools from kindergarten to twelfth grade. My schools weren't perfect, but they were good enough. Through school and through my afternoons reading at the library, I got the education I needed to go to college and get a job. And I am grateful for it.

From the first day I set foot in Harrisburg, one of my top priorities was supporting Pennsylvania's, and especially Philadelphia's, schools. After all, a person needs a good education to get a good job. Good schools and good jobs – those are the keys to good neighborhoods. I was committed to doing whatever I could to help the Philadelphia School District. I fought for increased education funding, and over the years I built good relationships with the Philadelphia Federation of Teachers, the Philadelphia School Board, and the superintendent. During my second House term, I even became an unlikely dealmaker and helped the School District and the Philadelphia Human Rights Commission work out a compromise on how to desegregate the schools. At the end of these contentious negotiations, the school board commended me for my efforts, and the *Philadelphia Inquirer* ran an editorial praising my work.

CB

True to my activist roots, I also stayed involved with my neighborhood schools. In 1981, we started Dwight Evans Career Days. We would bring professionals into elementary schools across the district so that kids could learn about different careers. Each year, I hosted a lunch for local principals at my district office and asked them what I could do to help. I listened hard to what these principals said – their feedback often drove my education policies in Harrisburg. With my position on the Appropriations Committee, one year I even got additional funding for my neighborhood schools to help them start tutoring programs and purchase much-needed equipment.

Despite our efforts to improve the neighborhood's schools, my constituents were not satisfied. Each year, parents came into my office and asked my staff to help them transfer their children to better schools outside the neighborhood. In hindsight, I can see that these parents were trying to do what my mother did when she changed our home address so that I could go to a better middle school – they were trying to exercise school choice within the limited options that were available to them. I always tried to help with transfers when I could, because I wanted my constituents to have the same options that politicians and wealthier families had. However, I was never comfortable with the whole transfer game. I knew it was an unsustainable solution to a very complex problem.

I was also conflicted. I had gone to my neighborhood schools, and even though they weren't perfect, they had prepared me for college and for a career. What had changed? Why were my constituents so unhappy? Sometimes I would look at parents and say, "You just have to work harder with what you have." They would stare back and ask, "Do you have children in these schools? Do you know what they're like?" I was doing everything I could to get more funding to make our schools better, but they were still struggling and parents still wanted out. Increased funding was important but that wasn't enough. Something had to change—we had to find a better way to run our schools and educate our kids.

Determined to figure out what that "better way" was, in the early 1990s I started reading and talking to every education expert I could find. I talked to Paul Hill, who wrote Reinventing Education. I met with Howard Fuller, a school choice advocate who was the superintendent of Milwaukee Public Schools. I talked to Ted Kolderie in Minnesota, who helped to develop the nation's first charter school law. During the 1996 Democratic National Convention, I skipped parties to sit down with a Chicago-based education reform group named Designed for Change and tour some local public schools to see what they were doing. I basically went on a crusade to learn as much as I could.

Through these conversations and through my reading, I became convinced that in Philadelphia, we had good people trapped in a bad system. The education system we had was designed for a world that no longer existed. Our schools were still functioning the way they had in the 18th and 19th centuries, with long summers and relatively short school days. The Philadelphia School District had a monopoly on public education in the city, and for a host of complicated reasons, it simply wasn't adjusting to the new marketplace quickly enough. And the stakes were higher than ever.

When I was growing up, the economy could absorb students who didn't get a great education. My dad dropped out of school in eighth grade, but after he served in the military, he was able to get a job that could support a family. But in the new economy, the post-manufacturing economy, that wasn't the case. When I worked as a job developer at the Urban League, I saw that if you didn't have a good education, you couldn't get a good job.

My constituents wanted change. They wanted a good education for their children, and they were looking to me for help, but I wasn't sure what I could do. How could I, as a state legislator, leverage my position to effect change? What more could I do to improve Philadelphia's public schools so that we could convince parents to stay in the city rather than move to the suburbs? In Philadelphia, it was the mayor who had the power to appoint school board members and influence the hiring of the district's superintendent. What could I do to change the system?

Through my research, I discovered that I could actually do a lot. In Pennsylvania, the state legislature is in charge of writing the Pennsylvania Public School Code, which governs how education is delivered throughout the Commonwealth. Through changing the state's school code, I could change the way the Philadelphia School District operated. In April of 1997, I introduced legislation that did just that. The City of Philadelphia School District Reform and Accountability Act (House Bill 1343) was designed to revolutionize the Philadelphia School District. It reformed the district's governance and management, strengthened accountability, improved teacher recruitment, and more.

At its core, H.B. 1343 was all about strengthening local control. Over the years I had seen that despite its best intentions, the Philadelphia School District's central office was often an impediment to getting things done. It was the central office that hired and fired teachers, and it was the central office that negotiated the union contract that laid out what those teachers would and wouldn't do during school hours. As a result, on many levels principals' hands were tied when it came to running their own schools. My bill took the power out of the central office and put it in the community. It gave principals the power to hire and fire teachers, and it created a parent-dominated council at every school that could hire and fire the principal. My theory was that if we empowered local principals and parents, we would end up with a more flexible, innovative and "child-centered" school district. I wanted a school district where debates over union contracts and other adult issues never got in the way of principals' and teachers' ability to do what was best for their students.

H.B. 1343 cemented my credentials as an education reformer; it was truly radical. At that point, no one had ever introduced legislation that would fundamentally restructure the Philadelphia School District. Needless to say, the Philadelphia Federation of Teachers was strongly opposed to my bill because it curtailed teachers' collective bargaining power. The union blasted my bill as a "shocking" proposal and a "political ploy." In the past, I had been one of the top recipients of the teachers union's political donations. After I introduced this bill, the teachers' union was so angry with me that it spent $150,000 and ran a candidate against me in the 1998 primary. When I ran for mayor the next year, union members rallied against me and carried signs that had an X over my face. But I wasn't afraid of the union's opposition. I knew that if we were going to keep people in the city, we had to fix the public schools. We had to do something radical.

Even though H.B. 1343 never passed the House, it did set the stage for me to join forces with John Perzel, Republican House Majority Leader, to pass Governor Tom Ridge's historic charter school bill in June of 1997. This law changed the education landscape in Pennsylvania by allowing parents and nonprofits to establish charter schools supported by public funds that were free from many of the constraints traditional public schools face. Although I was once skeptical of charter schools, the more I studied them the more I realized that creating charter schools in Pennsylvania was another way to give parents more control over the education of their children. By introducing the element of competition into the education sector, charter schools could help to improve the quality of public education overall.

Even though the charter school bill was a top priority for Ridge, getting it passed wasn't easy. A couple of Ridge's education reform proposals had already failed, so he knew he needed Democratic support if his charter school bill was going to go anywhere. I think the Ridge folks asked me to champion the bill in the House because my own education bill had shown them that I was serious about reform and that I could be a powerful ally. In return for my support, Ridge pledged to seriously consider my education bill. He also agreed to strip out a part of his bill that conflicted with my vision of how the Philadelphia School District should be restructured. The sight of me joining forces with Ridge was as surprising to people as the sight of President Obama and New Jersey Governor Chris Christie embracing each other in the wake of Hurricane Sandy in 2012. However, I was never hesitant to align myself with unlikely allies if I thought that by doing that, I could get things done.

Once I was on board, I took to the House floor and spoke in favor of the bill, praising it as "child-centered" legislation that would give parents much-needed options. With a nod towards my Democratic colleagues, I took care to point out that President Clinton himself supported charter schools. Even though Ridge's bill was not perfect, it was an important step forward. It was a dramatic finish: The Senate passed the bill late one night, and then sent it to the House. Around midnight, we adjourned for a caucus, where once again, I urged my colleagues to vote yes. We finally passed the bill by a vote of 137-57 at 3:38 a.m. on June 11, 1997. In the end, Rep. Anthony Hardy Williams and I succeeded in getting all but two of the Philadelphia Democrats to vote for it. And with that, we made history.

Even though I thought that opening charter schools in Pennsylvania was an important step, I never thought it was the only answer to our state's education problems. Education was much more complicated than that, and after the charter school bill passed, I kept fighting for other policies that could improve schools. I introduced legislation to extend student loan forgiveness to teachers who taught in urban or rural districts. I worked to create a neighborhood assistance tax credit for businesses that provided technology or training to urban schools. And I succeeded in getting the House to pass a bill that reduced class sizes in grades K-3. I wanted to tackle our state's education problems from every angle, and I never stopped trying to do that.

I also never forgot about my constituents, and all of the parents in my neighborhood who were desperate for better schools and better options. A few weeks after the charter school bill passed in Harrisburg, I was talking to Sharmain Matlock-Turner, who was the president of OARC's board. I looked at her and I asked, "What if we started our own charter school right here?" As we discussed the idea, we realized that this was our chance to give our kids the education they deserved. We called OARC, and it quickly agreed to take the lead in establishing a charter school to serve the West Oak Lane neighborhood. OARC did its research carefully – its staff members attended a charter school conference to learn how to put together an application, and they travelled to Massachusetts and Colorado to see charter schools in action. In February 1998, OARC's hard work paid off, and the Philadelphia Board of Education granted it a charter.

We moved quickly. I helped OARC's staff search for a location for the school. We soon found a vacant complex at the corner of Washington Lane and Stenton Avenue that fit the bill. Once a Cousin's Food Market and a Rite Aid Drug Store, this 41,000-square-foot building was filled with cobwebs, abandoned checkout counters, and old freezers. As we walked through it though, we knew we could make it something great. We were so excited we had an architect complete renderings for the building's renovation before we even signed the lease. Once the lease was finalized in mid-June, we had ten weeks to transform this vacant grocery store into a functioning school. It was a sprint from start to finish, but we got it done.

In September 1998, West Oak Lane Charter School (WOLCS) opened with 428 pupils in grades K-4 and twenty-six teachers. It was one of nine charter schools that opened in Philadelphia that fall. Even though we had achieved a remarkable success just by opening, we faced several challenges during that first year. In October, our principal resigned suddenly. We didn't have enough computers, and we had problems with school lunches. But we fixed these problems quickly. WOLCS has now been open for fourteen years and it has made adequate yearly progress (AYP) on state tests (as defined by the No Child Left Behind Act) for five years running. By contrast, only 13 percent of the Philadelphia School District's traditional schools made AYP during the 2011-2012 school year.

In helping to start WOLCS, I effectively took another step towards realizing my vision of a decentralized education system. Indeed, one of the keys to WOLCS' success was the amount of control its leaders had. Our principal was able to hire the teachers that he wanted. Our teachers were unionized, but it was the school itself, rather than the district's central office, that negotiated its union contract. As a result, WOLCS was able to offer its teachers performance-based incentives. The school's organizers, myself included, always knew that WOLCS' ability to control what happened within its doors was hugely important.

Despite WOLCS' achievements, I was keenly aware that our work was not done. WOLCS only went up to middle school. Once kids graduated from WOLCS, the exodus from the neighborhood's schools began again – students went on to high school at other charter schools and special admission schools throughout the city. These kids wanted to go anywhere except the high school in our own neighborhood, Martin Luther King High School. It wasn't hard to see why. For years, King had been plagued by violence and low performance. It was routinely on the School District's "persistently dangerous list," and it often felt like there were more King students on the street than there were in the classroom. At times, there were literally fires at the school.

Once again, I knew that if I wanted to keep families in the neighborhood, I had to find a way to make sure their kids could go to good schools from pre-school all the way through high school. Starting West Oak Lane Charter School was a big step forward, but it wasn't enough. We had to think bigger. I began to craft a vision for a high-quality education pipeline, a unified network of schools – both public charter schools and traditional public schools – that would share resources and that would be supported by strong community partnerships. Although I hadn't heard of it at the time, my thinking was very much in line with what Geoffrey Canada has tried to do with the Harlem Children's Zone. We both wanted to create a comprehensive network of support for children that would stretch from the cradle to college.

The first step in putting this vision into place was to find a partner who could oversee and manage all these schools. On the heels of Pennsylvania's charter school law, in 1998 Act 46 had officially given the Philadelphia School District the power contract with for-profit and non-profit entities to run schools. My thought was that if one nonprofit oversaw this whole education network in Northwest Philadelphia, then we could ensure that kids were properly prepared at every level and give principals the flexibility and power they needed to really move the needle in terms of student performance. Once again, my vision was all about taking control out of the central office and putting it in the community.

With this idea, I started talking to Rhonda Lauer, a longtime friend who had a wealth of education experience. Over the years, Rhonda had served as a teacher, principal, and superintendent. In her current role, she was running Foundations, Inc., a nonprofit that organized after-school programming for students. Foundations had worked in Northwest Philadelphia schools for years, and it had deep ties to the community. Even though Foundations had not run a school before, I was confident that with Rhonda in the lead, it could provide the management and oversight that our neighborhood schools network would need. However, Rhonda was resistant.

I first pitched my idea of a Foundations-run neighborhood

schools network to Rhonda when we were eating lunch together one day at a local diner. As we talked, I knew I had to get Rhonda to share my vision in order to make it a reality. After I finished speaking, she just looked at me and said: "Dwight, all you have to do is to send birthday cards to your constituents and you will get reelected. Why do you want to get involved with managing these schools? This is really messy stuff!" I knew it was messy, but I also knew that I had to do something to improve all these schools if I wanted our neighborhood to thrive. I knew Rhonda was the right person for this job, and so I kept talking to her until eventually, I sold her on my vision and she agreed to join me.

Once Rhonda was on board, our next step was to convince the Philadelphia School District to give Foundations control over fifteen northwest Philadelphia schools, spanning pre-K through 12th grade, with King as our lynchpin high school. We made our pitch to Philadelphia Mayor John Street and his administration just as he was focusing on his neighborhood transformation initiative. After my experience at WOLCS, I knew that in order to really change things, Foundations would need to have the power to choose its own principals and its own staff, and we negotiated hard to get that power.

Unfortunately Foundations was never really given the autonomy it needed to really realize our vision. The School District only agreed to let Foundations run a handful of schools it had wanted. Therefore even though Foundations got to manage King, it didn't get to manage many of the schools that fed into it. As a result, it couldn't ensure that all of King's students were properly prepared for high school. Additionally, the School District never really let Foundations fully control the schools it was allowed to run. For example, while Foundations could technically hire its own teachers, it could only hire them if they were already on the district's approved hire list. Despite the limitations and the difficulties we faced, we all tried to make the best of a less-than-perfect situation, especially when it came to turning King around. Helping Foundations manage King was like throwing a Hail Mary pass at the end of a football game when your team is down by four points. I knew the odds were against us, but I also knew that if we succeeded, that could make all the difference.

Foundations found out it would have control of King in August of 2003, which gave it very little time to prepare. The first thing Foundations did, along with my help, was to gather baseline data about the school's condition. Then we set about making changes. Our first priority was improving campus security and making the school a safe place. We also worked to change the perception of the school. We put up signs that said "Under New Management" because we wanted to make it clear to parents and teachers that this was a new day.

Foundations also tried to raise the bar in terms of performance. It implemented professional development and teacher training programs, increased the number of Advanced Placement classes, and started serving healthier food in the cafeteria. It even built a greenhouse at the school so that students could learn about urban agriculture. I was proud of what Foundations was doing, and I tried to support their efforts by keeping in contact with the Philadelphia superintendent and various politicians so that they knew what improvements were being made. I also tried to do what I could to improve King's environment. For example, through my relationship with the Philadelphia Symphony Orchestra, I was able to convince them to give their Martin Luther King Jr.

Day Concert at Martin Luther King High School. This quickly began one of the most popular events in the community – and the kids loved it.

As important as it was to change King internally, we also knew that in order to really give these kids a chance, we had to find ways to change their environments outside of the classroom as well. After all, if you can change the environment, you can change the behavior. That's where our community partners came in. OARC, for example, cleaned up Awbury Park so that students no longer had to walk through an unsafe area to get to school every day. OARC also worked with Foundations to create the Philadelphia Center for Arts and Technology (PCAT). At PCAT, King students and community members could take free classes in music, graphic design, computers, and more. These classes could open up a whole new world and a whole new career path for students.

Along those same lines, through my position on the Appropriations Committee, I got funding to start a Job Resource and Development Center (JRDC) at King. The JRDC's model was simple: If students went to class and participated in soft-skills trainings, the JRDC would help them get good-paying jobs after school hours. I loved this program because it reminded me of how I grew up – all those after-school jobs I had had motivated me to stay in school. I was hoping the JRDC would have the same impact. It did – the JRDC motived kids to stay in school and work hard.

At the end of the day, I think we all increasingly saw that education is not just about reading, writing and arithmetic. It is about empowering students to be productive citizens. Over time, our concept of a neighborhood schools network morphed into the Northwest Education Corridor. Our basic idea never changed, but our vision of an integrated school network bolstered by community supports only got stronger over time. We never stopped looking for innovative ways to prepare our kids to lead successful lives.

Over the years, Foundations made a lot of progress at King, despite the fact that it had to manage the school with one arm tied behind its back. First and foremost, it made King safer, and as a result, the school was removed from the School District's "persistently dangerous list." Students' math and reading scores increased by double digits, and more community organizations got involved at the school and committed to helping students succeed. That's not to say that everything was going perfectly. Despite the gains Foundations made, by 2010 fewer than 25 percent of King students were proficient in reading and math. King had made a lot of progress, but there was definitely still a long way to go. Unfortunately, Foundations never had the opportunity to take King as far as it could have. Despite my efforts to create a "child-centered" school district, adult issues and adult conflicts still got in the way.

The story of how Foundations' tenure at King came to an end stands out in my mind as one of the greatest disappointments of my career. Even though as I look back now I can honestly say that I would not have done anything differently, I am still frustrated by how it all worked out.

When Foundations' contract was up for renewal in January of 2011, the School District announced that King was going to go through the school district's "Renaissance Match" process and become a full-fledged charter school. As part of this process, a School Advisory Committee (SAC) made up of King parents, students, staff and community members would get to vote on which outside education management organization they thought should run King. Then, the school district's superintendent would review the SAC's decision before passing it along to the School Reform Commission (SRC) for final approval.

I was wary of this process from the very beginning. The Renaissance Match process treated King like it was an independent operation and seemed to ignore all of the community partnerships Foundations had formed over the years—partnerships that were now critical to the school's success. Additionally, there was no question that King's on-going struggles put Foundations in the defensive position. Still, I was hopeful everything would work out. Foundations had devoted a lot of time and resources to building a relationship with King's families, and I hoped that that and its vision would carry it through.

Unfortunately it didn't. After what I felt was an exclusive and biased deliberation period, King's SAC voted 8-1 to award King's charter to Mosaica, a for-profit company from Atlanta which had no ties to our neighborhood and lacked experience managing high schools. I was very upset. Just a couple of days earlier, a straw poll taken at a community meeting found that the majority of people there still wanted Foundations to run King. Despite this, the SAC was determined to go in another direction.

Although I respected the parents who served on the SAC, I was convinced that they had made the wrong decision. Many of these parents hadn't been active at King since the beginning of Foundations' time there, and therefore they couldn't see how much progress Foundations had made. Additionally, I wasn't sure how much these parents really knew about education reform and how it worked. After studying education reform for more than a decade, I knew that Mosaica could not lead King as well as Foundations could. Foundations knew this neighborhood, it had longstanding ties with other local nonprofits, and it had a comprehensive vision for the future. Mosaica, on the other hand, did not have pre-existing relationships with many of the neighborhood nonprofits that were now helping King's students. It had no sense of what we wanted to accomplish with the Northwest Education Corridor. If Mosaica took over now, I was sure that King's progress would stall and the school's parents and students would suffer as a result.

When I think something is important, I always speak out. Given how important King was to my neighborhood, I knew I had to fight for what I thought was right. After all, the SAC vote was just the first step in the process – it was never meant to be binding. So I shared my concerns with Arlene Ackerman, the School District Superintendent, and Bob Archie, the Chair of the SRC. Although Ackerman wasn't interested in keeping Foundations at King, Archie felt that I had an important perspective to share. With his permission, I personally pressed the SRC to keep Foundations at King. As I did so, I shared concerns I had heard about the lack of clarity and inclusiveness in the SAC's decision making process, and I highlighted how important Foundations was, not just to King, but to the Northwest Education Corridor as a whole. Despite my best efforts, in the end, the SRC still voted to let Mosaica take over King.

Right after the SRC's vote, Archie saw how upset I was. He pulled me into a room with the district's deputy superintendent, Leroy Nunery, and Mosaica's President, John Porter, in hopes that we could all find a way to work together going forward. At Archie's request, I passionately outlined why I thought we needed Foundations at King and how important Foundations was to my vision for the Northwest Education Corridor as a whole. After I spoke, Porter asked me repeatedly if I could work with Mosaica instead.

Given the stakes, I had to be honest. I had known Rhonda Lauer for decades, and I trusted her implicitly. You simply cannot replicate a relationship like that at the drop of hat. I didn't really know Mosaica, and the little I had learned about them did not make me want to work with them. I was committed to the neighborhood, and I would keep working to help these kids, but I wasn't going to partner with Mosaica to do it. Even though I made it clear that I wasn't going to work with him, I did wish Porter luck.

The next day, Porter sent an email to Superintendent Ackerman saying that Mosaica was withdrawing its bid to run King. In his email, Porter said that Mosaica was stepping down because he now understood that Foundations and myself had a comprehensive vision for King and its fellow neighborhood schools, and he did not want to interfere. Indeed, in his email, Porter even praised our plans for the Northwest Education Corridor by saying the following: "Although it is our belief that we are able to provide the educational services to turn around Martin Luther King High School, we also recognize that State Rep. Dwight Evans's extensive community plan provides more comprehensive strategies for tackling the myriad of issues that the Northwest community will face in the future including the education of students who attend this high school. We are confident in his ability to lead this aggressive approach to turn

CB

around the school which we believe is destined for academic greatness."

I was elated. As I told a local reporter later that day, I had been like a "bulldog with a bone" – I had made my case for Foundations to everyone and in the end, I had succeeded.

With Mosaica having dropped out, it seemed that everything was in place for Foundations to run King as a charter school during the next school year. Before the SRC held their final vote however, all hell broke loose. A few weeks after Mosaica dropped its bid, Philadelphia's local public radio station released a story describing how Archie had convened, in their words, "a pivotal, closed-door meeting to discuss the fate of a charter school deal potentially worth $60 million." I found this story to be somewhat ironic in that in March I had told that very same radio station that I had talked to Porter after the SRC's vote to share my concerns. I was always open about where I stood and I never tried to hide anything. But the media had a field day.

Soon every news outlet in town was writing stories criticizing our "secret" meeting with Porter after the SRC's vote. In the media's eyes, this was about money: Foundations' executives had donated to my campaign, and then I tried to help them get a charter worth $12 million a year. The truth is I could not have cared less about any donations Foundations' executives made to my campaign. I advocated for Foundations because I thought that was the right thing to do for King's parents and students. But the reporters never really explored the rationale behind my thinking. They might allude to the Northwest Education Corridor, but they never took the time to really explain what it was, what our plan was and why it mattered. Instead, newspapers like the *Philadelphia Daily News* ran editorials that said this was

CR

a case of "democracy vs. the power broker." In the media's eyes, the MLK SAC were the good guys, and I was the bad guy for challenging their decision.

As the media criticized my actions, people kept saying that I had a "strong interest" in Foundations. The truth is I had a strong interest in my neighborhood, and I advocated for Foundations because I thought it could do the best job of helping our students. Rhonda had warned me at the beginning that getting involved in managing schools could be messy, but I don't think I ever could have guessed just how messy it would be. Despite all the criticism I got for speaking out the way I did, I've never regretted fighting for what I thought was right. One of the deepest truths in politics is that if you are fighting for change, sometimes you're going to get hit. I never minded that, though – win or lose, I would always rather fight for what I believe in than stay on the sidelines.

As the media's firestorm grew more and more intense, Foundations concluded it was fighting a losing battle. Given the MLK SAC's continued opposition, and all of the media controversy surrounding Mosaica's decision to withdraw, Foundations saw that it would be nearly impossible for it to manage King going forward. So, it decided to withdraw its own bid. Instead of becoming a charter, King would once again be managed directly by the Philadelphia School District.

The hardest part of seeing Foundations lose King was the fact that all of us who had worked together for so long to turn this school around did not get to finish what we started. When I look back now, however, I can see that we did achieve a lot. Perhaps most importantly, our efforts helped advance the conversation about how to transform urban schools. No one had really tried

CB

to remake an existing school before, and to this day, few have gotten it right. But we tried our best and on many levels, we did make a real difference.

Sometimes people ask why I got so involved in how my neighborhood's schools were run. I certainly cannot think of any other legislator who was as involved in their local schools as I was. I got involved because I saw improving these schools as part of my core mission. Since well before I got elected to the state legislature, I was committed to doing whatever I could to improve the quality of life in my district and throughout the entire state. Working to improve local schools was a key component of achieving that goal. Unfortunately, it often seemed like I was too far out in front of the crowd for my ideas to stick.

Despite the disappointments and the struggles I've faced over the years, I am hopeful for the future. Today, nearly 60,000 children in the city of Philadelphia attend charter schools. Sixteen years after Governor Ridge and I banded together to enact the historic charter school law, now many Philadelphia parents do have a choice when it comes to deciding where to send their children to school. Additionally, the conversation around education in this city is changing.

In 2012, the Boston Consulting Group, a well-known national management consulting firm, was commissioned to develop recommendations on how the School District could improve its management and address its growing budget deficit. At the School District's request, the report focused in part on how to "increase school autonomy" and use "parents and teachers as the agents of school change." These are the very issues I sought to address in my 1997 education reform bill. Years after I was heavily criticized for talking about decentralizing the school district, this idea is a very real and very credible part of the conversation. While I sorely wish that these ideas could have entered the mainstream earlier, the conversations that we are now having about education in Philadelphia give me hope that we are moving in the right direction.

A Leap of Faith: Launching the Fresh Food Financing Revolution

When I was growing up, my family usually shopped at a big supermarket on Cecil B. Moore Avenue named Best Market. It had a wide variety of food, including tons of fresh fruits and vegetables, all at reasonable prices. But by the early 2000s, Best Market had closed, along with all the other good groceries. If you wanted fresh food, you had to drive out of the neighborhood. If you didn't have a car, you were just out of luck. You had to go down the street to the corner convenience store and take what you could get. The quality of food at these stores was often abysmal.

When a supermarket closes, a community like mine loses dozens of good paying jobs. As someone who is obsessed with revitalizing urban neighborhoods, I knew that if I wanted to jump-start a local economy, I had to help bring groceries and supermarkets back to these neighborhoods.

By the early 2000s, the lack of supermarkets in urban areas was becoming a hot national issue, especially in Philadelphia. We had the second lowest number of supermarkets per capita of any city in the country. Some neighborhoods had started seeing protests over the lack of fresh food. The Food Trust, a Philadelphia nonprofit, put together a map of Philadelphia's "food deserts," areas where residents did not have access to

೦ಽ

fresh, healthy food. It found a strong correlation between the communities with the fewest supermarkets and the communities with the highest rates of obesity and heart disease. As I sat through one of The Food Trust's presentations, I saw that having supermarkets in a neighborhood isn't just a matter of economic health — it's a matter of personal health. If we could find a way to bring quality food stores back to these neighborhoods, we could help families lead healthier lives and create the synergy needed to attract other private investment. Just like the convention center, the importance of finding ways to lure groceries back to the inner city was a no-brainer to me. The key was finding out how to do it.

Working with The Food Trust and other local nonprofits, I convened a meeting where we asked grocery operators, big and small: What it would take to lure you back into inner city neighborhoods and other under-served areas across the state? The grocers said that they were open to building new stores in the city, but they could never get the private-lender financing they needed to cover their hefty construction and start-up costs. In the suburbs, where there were supermarkets on every corner, land was cheap and people were rich. In the city, land was expensive and people were poor. As a result, it was next to impossible to get the capital needed to build a new store.

Through OARC, I had seen what it took to finance redevelopment and construction projects in the inner city. As I listened to these grocers, I saw that if we could find a way to reduce their startup and construction costs, they could launch viable operations. This was an area where a small interjection of government funds could lead to a big payoff. If we could get state funding to help finance grants and tax credits that

156

would lower supermarkets' development and start-up costs, we could help them open new stores in under-served areas that would pay dividends for years to come.

So in 2004 I decided to take action. Through my position on the Appropriations Committee, I set aside $10 million in state funding to create the Pennsylvania Fresh Food Financing Initiative (FFFI). Over the next three years, I would direct $10 million a year towards helping businesses start and expand groceries in under-served areas. It was an ambitious plan–especially since Democrats were the minority party in the House. But I never doubted I could get the funding because I knew that Governor Ed Rendell was my ally. Rendell had known me for years, and he knew that I was a serious lawmaker who wanted to do serious things. When I told him that something was important to me, he generally trusted my instincts. And the Fresh Food Financing Initiative was not only important to me – it was important to him as well.

Even with Rendell's support, however, I knew that I couldn't create the FFFI using a stand-alone piece of legislation because the legislative process is a meat grinder. If the FFFI was its own bill, the legislative vultures would have tried to put in various stipulations and restrictions on it. They would have picked the FFFI apart before it ever got launched. What we needed to do was to provide state funding without micromanaging how that funding would be used. There was no better way to do that than by using a WAM. And so when I was at the table negotiating the budget, I made it clear that the FFFI was my priority. That was what I wanted to fund with my slice of the budget pie. My fellow appropriators deferred to me and we got the funding we wanted. The FFFI's success is yet another example of how we used WAMS és

to meet pressing needs, create jobs, and spark private economic development. Once again, by using the state budget, I was able to drive policy outcomes.

Creating a new program like the FFFI is a lot like dancing – it can work beautifully if you find the right partner. The cabinet-level Pennsylvania Department of Community and Economic Development would have a major role to play in dispersing state funding and overseeing the program's administration. In order for the program to really take off, however, I knew that the FFFI needed private capital and private sector support. In other words, it needed to be a private-public partnership. With that framework, we could use state funding to launch the program and private sector funding and expertise to sustain it.

The Food Trust would clearly have a key role. With its extensive research and mapping initiative, it could pinpoint Pennsylvania's "food deserts" so we could target our funding. I also wanted the Urban Affairs Coalition to be a part of the conversation. The UAC had been founded in 1968 in response to a wave of unrest and rioting in other major American cities, and I knew it could ensure that minority and women-owned businesses were able to take advantage of the investments we were making. The final crucial piece of the puzzle was finding an organization that could provide the financial expertise needed to make this whole operation work, an organization that could structure the various financial packages needed to get these groceries off the ground. And for that, there was no one better than The Reinvestment Fund (TRF).

TRF was started in 1985 by Jeremy Nowak, a Philadelphian who is a civic entrepreneur in the fullest sense of the word. By securing capital—from socially conscious investors, religious and

158

civic groups, financial institutions, foundations, and the public sector—over the last twenty-seven years, TRF had invested more $1.1 billion in neighborhood revitalization throughout the Mid-Atlantic region. It had financed the construction of nearly 20,000 units of affordable housing and helped to create, renovate and preserve more than 9.5 million square feet of commercial space. Today, it is one of the most respected community development financial institutions in the country. As I laid out my vision for FFFI, I knew that no one understood how to use public funds to leverage private investments better than Jeremy. I had known him for nearly a decade, and I had seen both his character and his success. I knew he could deliver the outcomes I was looking for. So I called him and said, "If I get you $30 million in state funding to finance the construction of supermarkets, can TRF raise private funding to triple it?"

"Absolutely," he answered.

And that was our team. Under the leadership of TRF, the Food Trust and the Urban Affairs Coalition, the Fresh Food Financing Initiative took off. Far beyond simply tripling the state's initial $30 million investment, TRF secured an additional $146 million for the FFFI before it was all over. The partnership worked just as I had hoped it would: The Food Trust identified areas of need and took the lead in raising awareness about FFFI among supermarket operators statewide. The Urban Affairs Coalition reached out to minority and women-owned businesses that were interested in becoming supermarket developers and helped supermarket operators connect with the community and find qualified employees. TRF put together the financial packages needed to launch new operations and expand existing ones. These packages could include everything from pre-development grants to low-interest loans that could help store operators with land acquisition, equipment financing, construction, employee recruitment, and training costs. Supporting all of our efforts were the business owners themselves, who took the initiative to apply for funding to expand their operations or launch new ones.

Providing FFFI with $30 million in state funding was a leap of faith, but it was a well-informed leap of faith, because I knew the people and the organizations in charge of the program's implementation. I knew Jeremy at TRF, I knew Sharmain Matlock-Turner at the Urban Affairs Coalition, and I knew Duane Perry at The Food Trust. I knew I could trust them. They all shared my vision and my passion, and they had the technical expertise and relationships needed to put it into action. I didn't tell Jeremy or The Food Trust where to put supermarkets. I just told them to call me for the groundbreakings. I trusted their expertise.

Even before FFFI was approved, I met with Jeff Brown, a fourth-generation grocer who owned the ShopRite Supermarket chain. Once he got wind of our idea, Jeff made his own leap of faith: He began rehabilitating an old supermarket in southwest Philadelphia even before we had the funding set aside. That was risky, but he trusted that I would deliver on my promises. I in turn was determined not to let Jeff down. We did come through right in time, and the FFFI was able to give Jeff a grant for his project as it neared completion. When Jeff and I met, it was a case of a political entrepreneur meeting a civic entrepreneur. We were two sides of the same coin, and we each needed each other to achieve our goals.

Jeff's before-the-funding actions were critical to the entire program because we needed a quick success story from a public relations standpoint. It was one thing to talk about the FFFI in theory, but with Jeff's store we had tangible proof that our idea could work. The media picked up on it, and favorable stories were written about the new grocery coming to Fifty-Second Street and Lancaster Avenue. The store at was an instant success, and it catapulted the FFFI to the forefront. By 2013, ShopRite had opened five other groceries. They have now started offering banking services in their stores, and one store even has a health clinic. Each store is profitable, and ShopRite is now Philadelphia's leading supermarket chain.

Over the six years the FFFI was active, eighty-eight different applicants in thirty-four Pennsylvania counties received loans or grants to expand their stores or start new ones in under-served areas. The program helped finance a large supermarket in North Philadelphia and small groceries in rural areas. The FFFI's investments also helped to support more than 5,000 jobs, and they provided nearly half a million Pennsylvanians with better access to fresh food. FFFI only financed supermarkets and groceries that could sustain themselves economically over the long term.

The FFFI was the first statewide program that was devoted to developing supermarkets in under-served areas. As the program's success grew, it attracted a lot of attention. The Harvard Kennedy School recognized the FFFI twice as one of the most innovative public policy programs in the country. The Centers for Disease Control and Prevention gave the FFFI its "Pioneering Innovation" award. Soon, leaders from other states were coming to Pennsylvania to study what we were doing so that they could replicate our efforts. California, New York, New Jersey, Louisiana and Illinois all have programs modeled after the

FFFI. The Food Trust is now working with local organizations in eleven other states to help them develop policies that could help improve communities' access to fresh food.

I've always wanted to take things to scale. If a certain policy or program worked in my neighborhood, I wanted to find ways that we could replicate that good throughout the city. And if it worked at the city level, I wanted to elevate it to the state level. And if it worked at the state level, I wanted to spread our lives and our programs nationwide. After all, one of the best elements of our federalist system of government is that smaller, local programs can grow to have a national impact. When I had a good idea, I was always on the lookout for opportunities to talk to other people about what I was doing and the impact it was having.

One night when I was in DC in May 2009, I had a golden opportunity to do exactly that. Just as I was walking out of my downtown hotel, I ran into Michael Strautmanis, a senior adviser to President Obama whom I had met during the 2008 campaign. We stopped to chat, and I told him about the FFFI's success. He was impressed and interested to learn more. The minute our brief conversation was over, I called my staff and told them to forward background information on the program to Strautmanis. After all, here was the chance to elevate our idea to the national level. We had to take advantage of it. A series of emails quickly turned into a meeting with the big guns in Washington.

Just a month later, I went to the White House to discuss the details of how the FFFI was created, how it worked, and what its impact had been. Accompanying me were Sharmain, Jeremy, Jeff Brown and Patrick Burns, the CEO of the Fresh Grocer chain, and others. It was very important to us to have Jeff and

Pat there because they were the operators who had made it all work. As businessmen, they could provide a firsthand account of how FFFI financing helped make it economically viable to build a supermarket in an under-served area. The timing was perfect, because the First Lady wanted to tackle America's obesity crisis, and the FFFI fit into that platform. We were well organized, we had access to the right people, and we were able to get the FFFI on Mrs. Obama's national agenda.

Some might say that my bumping into Strautmanis and the events that followed were a stroke of luck. I don't believe in luck. Our success in elevating the FFFI to the national level was a story of hard work meeting opportunity. Part of being a policy entrepreneur is constantly being on the lookout for opportunities to make a change and being prepared to seize those opportunities when they appear. That is how you get things done.

On February 19, 2010, Mrs. Obama unveiled her signature "Let's Move" campaign in Philadelphia and announced that the Obama Administration was planning to launch its own Healthy Food Financing Initiative, modeled after Pennsylvania's program. The First Lady began the day by visiting Fresh Grocer's new supermarket at Progress Plaza in North Philadelphia— the very shopping center that my childhood hero, Reverend Leon Sullivan, built decades ago. Before this grocery opened, this neighborhood hadn't had a food store for more than ten years. When this $15 million Fresh Grocer opened in 2009, it created 270 jobs, 75 percent of which were filled by people who lived within a two-mile radius. This Fresh Grocer supermarket was a perfect example of what we had hoped the FFFI would accomplish.

Then Mrs. Obama went to Fairhill Elementary School to

unveil the Obama Administration's plans for the Healthy Food Financing Initiative (HFFI). She said: "We know it won't be easy to solve this obesity crisis, but if there's anyone out there who doubts that it can be done, I would urge them to come to Philadelphia and see what you have done here." Under the federal HFFI, U.S. Departments of Agriculture and Treasury have allocated hundreds of millions of dollars towards helping the private sector increase the availability of healthy food in underserved areas. Indeed, when you total up the investments that have been made by the federal, state and local governments, as well as private foundations, more than $1 billion has been invested in fresh food financing programs and tax credit initiatives. Never in my wildest dreams would I have imagined that Pennsylvania's FFFI would spur more than $1 billion in fresh food financing.

Not only did the FFFI help to launch a national movement, in the City of Philadelphia it has also helped to stem one of the greatest public health crises of our time: childhood obesity. In 2012, the Robert Wood Johnson Foundation reported that Philadelphia's childhood obesity rate dropped by five percent from 2006 to 2010. Most remarkably, the largest decline in obesity was among the very minority students who are often at the greatest risk of being overweight. This is one of the first times that researchers have seen a decrease in the childhood obesity rate. While the FFFI was only one of several healthy eating initiatives in Philadelphia in recent years, I have no doubt that it has helped to spur positive change.

In working to implement the FFFI, I drew on the broad base of knowledge I had amassed over three decades of legislating. I identified the problem, I sought out a solution, I put together a team, and we executed my vision. With good organization and natural synergy–and by that I mean the meshing of several different entities to produce a result greater than the sum of their individual effects—we helped pave the way for the FFFI to go from a Pennsylvania program to a national initiative. Three people standing under an apple tree may not be able to reach the fruit. But if two of them stand on the other one's shoulders, they can.

Around the same time I was coming up with the FFFI, I was also focused on the great irony in the economics of poverty: The poorer you are, the more things cost. This is an inescapable fact of life that most people who have never lived below the poverty line cannot understand. Not only did families have to pay more for food at poorly stocked convenience stores, there were many other manifestations of this cruel irony. Poorer families face higher fees and higher interest rates when they borrow money or take out a credit card. They have to use laundromats because they don't have washers and dryers at home, and they have to use check-cashing services because they don't have bank accounts.

Let's step back a few years to the beginning of the new millennium. Pennsylvania's economy was not where anyone wanted it to be. The 2001 recession hit the state hard, and no one felt it more than the state's working families. All across the state, there were hundreds of thousands of families who, despite their best efforts, could not move beyond living paycheck to paycheck. I grew up in a Working-Class family, and I knew how perilous financial security could be. In the wake of yet another recession, I wanted to find ways that we could help families increase their incomes and build their financial assets.

છ

Therefore, just like I did with charter schools and so many other issues, I studied the issue of financial security from every angle. On the basis of my reading and my conversations, I began to form ideas around ways that the state could expand its student loan forgiveness programs and make it easier for start-up businesses to succeed. With these ideas circulating in my head, in June 2003 I convened a small team of fellow legislators and community leaders to travel to the National Council of State Legislature's (NCSL) working conference on "Helping Working Families in Tight Budget Times." There we exchanged ideas and information with ten other state teams on how to help working families build their financial assets without spending a lot of state money. It was an invigorating trip, and we left with a list of data we wanted to collect, polices that we wanted to study, and actions we wanted to take to help working families.

After we did a little research, we decided to host a retreat of our own for Pennsylvania state legislators and Philadelphia City Council members in the fall. With the NCSL's help, we organized a retreat in October of 2003 that featured national experts from the Annie E. Casey Foundation and the Corporation for Enterprise Development, as well as local experts. Our goal was simple: We wanted to engage key Pennsylvania policy makers in developing initiatives that would help working families and small businesses. Even though Pennsylvania already had a number of good policies on the books , many of them were not being enforced or implemented correctly and therefore were not as effective as they could be. There was work to be done and progress to be made. I made sure my staff kept a record of what was discussed, and after the conference we sent a summary report outlining key points from different sessions, different policy ideas, and next steps to all the participants. I wanted to make sure that everyone there remembered what was said and discussed. We were gaining momentum and we wanted to keep it going.

At this point, one of the best ways to keep moving forward was to develop a statewide task force that could investigate in-depth how the state could improve its policies. There were many different agencies and organizations that could and should be involved in addressing this problem, and a task force could keep the lines of communication and coordination open. To do this, we needed the help of the big guy himself, Governor Rendell.

But like all governors, Rendell had a million items on his agenda at any one time. It was up to me to focus his attention to move the ball forward, but I knew that the governor would like the idea of a task force once I told him about it because he cared about working families, and he cared about the state's economy. So I scheduled a meeting with the governor and made my pitch.

When he gave his annual budget address in February 2004, he included the following lines: "We can do even more to help our struggling citizens improve their financial stability....Rep. Dwight Evans came to me with a great idea. He suggested that I appoint a Task Force on Working Families to use the breadth of our state agencies to help our citizens become better financial consumers, to help families build assets and increase income. I plan to create that task force this month." At the end of April, Rendell issued an executive order creating the task force and appointed me and state Banking Secretary William Schenck as co-chairs.

We brought together a diverse group of more than sixty people that included everyone from other legislators and other cabinet members to bankers, clergy, and community organizers. It was critical that we involved community leaders because they were on the ground working to help families every day, so they knew what working families needed, and they could raise families' awareness of the help that was available. We divided the group into four issue-based committees that focused on building assets, improving financial education, increasing incomes and preventing financial abuse. Then we had twenty-four open discussions all across the state so that we could hear from everyday citizens about the challenges they faced and the policies they thought could make a difference.

As we travelled across the state, we met people like Michelle, whose story we included in the final report:

> Michelle is a teacher in Philadelphia. Her husband is a police officer. Yet, they're struggling to make ends meet. They were awe struck and delighted at the birth of their new baby, but now they find themselves financially strapped because the costs of newborn care have amplified the financial strain resulting from Michelle's maternity leave. The monthly bills are late, and the mortgage is overdue.

It was important to include these personal stories in the report because they made the issues we were talking about concrete. They provided our target audience with a real-life example of why we needed to connect families to quality education and why we needed to crack down on predatory lending. They helped make these issues real even to people who may not have a first-hand knowledge of them.

Now it's true that government loves to write reports.

Oftentimes, these reports don't do anything but gather dust on crowded shelves. But our final report, which we appropriately named Dollars and Sense, really did make a difference because when we wrote it, we had the people who could put our ideas into action in the room with us. As the *Philadelphia Daily News* said in an editorial, the report was "'a blueprint for action' that succinctly shows who needs to do what to achieve these goals." We included a list of action steps for everyone from the governor down to local financial services providers. Painfully aware that the state's budget was growing ever tighter, we also took care to point out that many of our recommendations would have little or no cost. Our ideas included everything from encouraging financial professionals to volunteer in financial education efforts to helping community organizations better publicize the Earned Income Tax Credit. We made sure to include a list of the state's current programs so that we could show that our new proposals would not duplicate them.

As a result of our report, we were able to get additional funding for Pennsylvania's Family Savings Account program, which encouraged low-income families to save money by using state dollars to match 50 percent of their savings, up to $1,000 over two years. The Department of Banking took new steps to regulate payday lenders who often preyed on the poor. We increased funding for the Self-Employment Assistance program, which helped unemployed individuals launch their own business ventures. And of course we laid the groundwork for our biggest success – the Pennsylvania Fresh Food Financing Initiative, a great idea that became a national model.

I went to Harrisburg in 1981 because I wanted to change people's lives for the better. I was frustrated by my inability to win election as governor or mayor, so I had to figure out a way to be effective. By my third decade in the Pennsylvania House, I knew how to get the executive branch to do what I wanted done. As chairman of the Appropriations Committee, I used the power of the purse to change the ways things were done. And in this way I was able to act as an executive from my seat in the legislature.

In his 2012 book *The Best Job in Politics,* Alan Rosenthal, the professor of public policy at Rutgers University's Eagleton Institute of Politics, says, "If you're governor, you are the quarterback calling the plays. The power of the individual members of the legislative branch is far less."

With all due respect to Mr. Rosenthal, a legislator CAN be a powerful force. Over the decades, I figured out how to use the tools I had at my disposal to get the executive to share my vision and make it reality. By picking the right partners and forming the right relationships, in many ways I became an executive policy maker from my legislative seat. From my viewpoint, the legislative branch, not the executive, is the permanent government. During the time that I have been in office, Pennsylvania has had six different governors. They have come and gone, but I have stayed.

Politics Is a Contact Sport

I have spent thirty-three years in the state legislature. Thirty-three years. Those years have been more rewarding and exciting than I ever could have imagined when I first ran for the State House at the age of twenty-five. People often ask me–how did you do what you did? How did you become the first African-American and the youngest member ever to be elected to chairman of the House Appropriations Committee? How did you kick start the Fresh Food Financing Initiative and elevate it to the national level? How did you rally the votes needed to get the Pennsylvania Convention Center built back in 1986? How did you do it?

In my eyes, the answer is simple: hard work. I have completely dedicated my life to my work. Since I was twenty-two years old, public service has been my pride and my joy. For most of my life, I have worked twelve hours a day, seven days a week. No matter what I'm doing, I never stopped thinking about the challenges facing my community and how we can tackle them. In my free time, I've devoured books on public policy and traveled to conferences to pick the brains of the brightest leaders around the country. I've constantly been on the lookout for new ideas for how to make government better. When Philadelphia's crime rate spiked in the 1990s, I went to New York to figure out what we could do to bring it down. I have never thought that any problem, big or small, was a problem that could not be solved.

In addition to a willingness, and a desire, to work hard, I have also always had a vision for what I wanted to accomplish. From day one, I knew that my mission in life was to help create strong, vibrant communities filled with good jobs, safe neighborhoods and successful schools.

As a child, I lived in a strong community, one in which everybody worked and neighbor looked after neighbor. After riots and recessions and years of urban decay, I saw signs that that strong community was fading away. I saw them in the abandoned factories that lay throughout north Philadelphia, in the struggles of the unemployed Philadelphians I tried to help while working at the Urban League, and in the eyes of frustrated youth who kept getting into trouble because "there wasn't anything better to do." Our neighborhoods were struggling, and it was up to us, as active citizens, to do whatever we could do to turn it around. My drive to strengthen my community took from me from being a neighborhood activist to being a ward leader to being a state representative. It has been an amazing journey.

Until I sat down to write this book, I never took much time to sit back and reflect on my life. I was too busy working. Now that I have taken the time to look back, I am proud of what I have helped to do. I am proud that Ogontz Plaza is filled with stores that provide good paying jobs for neighborhood residents. I am proud that tens of thousands of Philadelphia children are now getting a great education in local charter schools. I am proud that the Pennsylvania Convention Center, the Avenue of the Arts and countless other projects we funded with WAMS and RACP money have revitalized Philadelphia and helped draw new residents to the city. I'm proud that I have been able to play a part in making Philadelphia and Pennsylvania a better place.

I am also very much aware that I could have never done any of this without others' help. In the public sector, change is always a team effort. Whether I was trying to pass a law or start a nonprofit, my ability to make a difference always depended on my ability attract others' support. After all, OARC would have never taken off without the support of West Oak Lane's business and community leaders. The Fresh Food Financing Initiative would have never succeeded without the work of The Food Trust, the Reinvestment Fund and the Urban Affairs Coalition. Time and time again, the key to success was finding the right partners and getting them to share my goals.

I view myself as a policy entrepreneur, a person who is constantly working to use the levers of power to bring about positive and permanent change. Time and time again I ran the same game plan: I identified the problem, explored all solutions, found the best possible solution, and helped bring about that solution with my power. As I did this, I never forgot that politics is a human capital game, and to play it well you have to know and understand who people are. So I always really tried to know and understand my colleagues and my constituents. Ultimately, to get things done you have to have an open mind and a willingness to learn. And most importantly you have to be able to ask people for what you want.

My career has been very rewarding, but it has had its frustrations too. My greatest frustration has been my inability to get elected to higher office. I was defeated in the Democratic

CR

primaries for lieutenant governor in 1986, for governor in 1994 and for mayor of Philadelphia in 1999 and 2007. My losses were decisive. My major problem was that the campaign style that served me so well in my district –door-to-door, face-to-face– did not work on bigger electoral stages. I always thought that if I had the opportunity, I could have been a great executive. But the first rule of political science is to get elected, and I was unable to do that on citywide and statewide platforms.

During these campaigns, I was constantly at odds with my political consultants, who said I spoke in "Legis-ese" rather than in the appealing sound-bites that are so much a part of modern television campaigning. When I ran for governor in 1994, one adviser wanted me to put on a Ronald Reagan mask to drive home a political point. I thought the gimmick was belittling to me and the former president, so I refused to do it. In the 2007 mayoral primary, my consultants kept urging me to run hard-hitting attack ads. I declined. I didn't want to win by tearing down the other candidates – I wanted to win by selling other people on my ideas and getting them to share my vision for the city. It was very frustrating. I felt that if people could hear what I was saying, they would support me. I kept asking myself, How do I get my message across? How do I connect with voters on a larger stage? In the process of writing this book, I've come to realize that I missed many opportunities to explain myself better. For example, in 1997, it never occurred to me to use the story of how my mother changed our address when I was entering nine grade so I could attend a better school to help explain why I thought charter schools were so important.

Even though I never succeeded in winning my campaigns for higher office, all those campaigns did serve a purpose.

For example, my campaign for lieutenant governor in 1986 introduced me to voters statewide and laid the groundwork for my successful run for chairman of the Appropriations Committee four years later. The key to politics, and perhaps the key to life, is to always find ways to work with what you have. And that's what I did. Although I was never elected to the executive branch, I found ways to become an "executive legislator." As chairman of the Appropriations Committee, I mastered the state budget and learned how to use it to influence how agencies were run and programs were implemented. I took the tools that were available to me, and I made the most of them.

Today, it makes me sad that many Americans have lost their faith in government and the political process. A lot of this disillusionment comes from pure frustration. People look at the political gridlock and political posturing in Harrisburg and Washington, DC and wonder why their representatives cannot get anything done.

Part of the reason why there is so much gridlock in Harrisburg these days is that many of the tools of the trade, tools that helped us move important bills through the process, have fallen by the wayside. For example, in 2011, Pennsylvania Governor Tom Corbett banned WAMs. At the time, he argued that WAMs were a waste of taxpayer money and that they should be eliminated.

Obviously, I have a very different view of WAMs. In my eyes, WAMs were the grease that enabled controversial measures to move through the legislature and helped good projects get much-needed funding. Without WAMs, we would have never gotten some of the votes we needed to get the convention center built.

Without WAMs, Charlie King and Old Tyrone Township would never have gotten clean water. Without WAMs, the Fresh Food Financing Initiative would have never gotten off the drawing board. If a program as innovative as the FFFI had had to go through the full legislative process, it would have been weighed down by a thousand different conditions and stipulations. As it was, by funding the FFFI with a WAM, we were able to ensure that nonpartisan experts like Jeremy Nowak at TRF could implement the program the way they saw fit.

In the budget hearings I held across Pennsylvania in the late 2000s, I heard from everyday citizens how WAMs, RACP and other state investments improved their lives for the better. Now much of that has been thrown out the window. Under the guise of "fiscal responsibility," Pennsylvania leaders have stopped making smart investments in our state's future. In my eyes, that is not responsible at all.

In addition to the gridlock that has gripped many state capitals nationwide, another reason many Pennsylvanians have grown suspicious of politicians is due to several political scandals that have gripped the state over the last decade. When I became Appropriations chairman in 1990, I was part of a youth movement in the Pennsylvania General Assembly that saw new leadership emerging to replace the Old Guard. It was truly a sea change. Sadly, many of my colleagues in the legislative leadership during these years fell by the wayside and ended up with prison terms for offenses connected to their public offices. Many of these former colleagues were instrumental in enacting important new laws for Pennsylvania, but these positive actions have been overshadowed by their misdeeds and downfalls.

Senator Vince Fumo, whom I was never close to and

frequently clashed with, is serving a five-year prison term on federal corruption charges. Rep. John Perzel–the Republican floor leader, former speaker, and part of the Gang of Five—was sentenced to two-and-a-half to five years on state charges of conflict of interest, theft and conspiracy. I was a close ally and friend of Rep. Mike Veon, the former House Democratic Whip, and was greatly saddened when he was imprisoned for charges related to using taxpayer-paid bonuses to reward state workers for campaign efforts. Rep. Bill DeWeese, a former House speaker, is serving time for theft, conspiracy and conflict of interest for using staff and resources for his political and personal benefit.

I look at them, and the others who went to prison, as the Legislature's Lost Generation. These men were talented politicians but at some point, they all lost their way. I always felt different from them because they weren't as obsessed as I was with the idea of not letting down myself, my family, and my constituents. As an African-American, I was always determined to be doubly above reproach. Given how few African-Americans there were in key leadership positions in state government, I wanted to make sure that I didn't poison anyone else's chances by abusing the power that had been given to me. I never forgot that strong sense of right and wrong that my grandmother instilled in me as a child. Every day, I do my best to honor her legacy and her expectations.

A common denominator in the fates of the Lost Generation is that they used public funds and resources for their own political gain. From the very beginning, I instinctively knew that this was wrong. When I took office I set up a firewall between my public duties and my political needs, because that was the right thing to do. I always kept my feet on the ground, and I never forgot that

Cℬℨ

I serve at the will of the people and I have a sacred responsibility to honor their trust.

It frustrates me to no end that in countless articles, reporters have looped me in with DeWeese, Fumo, and others and assumed that I did exactly what they did. I didn't. I never wanted to use my position for personal or political gain and I never did. After all, my personal needs are small — I live in a house that I paid $106,000 for in 1992. I still owe $40,000 on the mortgage. I don't have a house at the shore, or in the Poconos. I was always far more interested in making a difference in my community than living an extravagant lifestyle.

It seems that the word "politician" has taken on such a negative connotation that it's almost an accusation. Large numbers of Americans feel alienated from politicians as a class. But we're not all the same. There are good politicians and bad politicians, just like there are good lawyers and bad lawyers, good reporters and bad reporters, and so on. If you're a good politician, you can compromise without abandoning moral principles. Indeed, that is exactly how many of our nation's most well-respected and transformative leaders have made history.

There's an old movie called *Mr. Smith Goes to Washington*. In it, a virtuous young man played by Jimmy Stewart goes to the U.S. Senate and is appalled by the politics of the place, because it contradicts his idealistic views of people like Thomas Jefferson and Abraham Lincoln. Hollywood almost always gets history wrong, and it certainly did in this case. Jefferson and Lincoln were not ivory-tower idealists – they were shrewd politicians who wanted to get things done.

As a state legislator, a congressman and a president, Abraham Lincoln showed time and time again that he knew how to line up votes for controversial bills, and he knew how to mobilize the public's support. Some historians have tried to paint Lincoln as an above-it-all saint, but the fact is he was a politician through and through. I always loved how the great American essayist H.L. Mencken once debunked the suggestion that Lincoln was not a politician: "What could be more absurd? Lincoln, in point of fact, was a practical politician of long experience and high talents, and by no means cursed with inconvenient ideals." Lincoln was well-schooled in the power of persuasive leadership, and he never hesitated to exercise his power for the greater good.

For years, I've been reading Robert Caro's great four-volume biography of Lyndon Johnson. LBJ is my political hero. To be sure, Johnson ran some rough campaigns, and he engaged in some tactics that I never would have used. But I have always respected how LBJ used his power to change our nation for the better. After all, LBJ was the man who brought us the Civil Rights Act of 1964, legislation that added some one million African-Americans to the voter rolls. He enacted Head Start and Medicaid. He brought millions of low-income workers under the protection of the minimum wage law, and the nation experienced strong economic prosperity.

LBJ did not achieve these historical legislative victories through using inspiring rhetoric. No, he achieved them by mobilizing political power in a manner seldom seen before or since. In other words, what made LBJ so successful is that he blended practical politics with his idealism.

Throughout my career, I have tried to do the same thing. In my eyes, that is what being a policy entrepreneur is all about. It is often said that politics is the art of the possible. That's true, but with enough energy, skill and dedication, it can also be the art of the impossible. LBJ proved that with the Civil Rights Act.

In 2004, after I succeeded in getting state money to combat youth violence, Tom Ferrick Jr., a well-known political journalist, wrote a column praising my efforts in the *Philadelphia Inquirer*. These words meant a great deal to me because they portrayed me as the type of leader that I have always aspired to be:

> Let us now praise Dwight Evans. Time and again, the state legislator from West Oak Lane has led the way to finding new answers to old problems in a smart and substantive way.
>
> He's also got the political moxie to break with tradition so that, instead of just talking about those problems, he actually devises solutions. He did it again this week. On Wednesday, Evans hosted a news conference at the Philadelphia District Attorney's Office, where $4.2 million in state grants was announced for new programs to reduce youth violence. But the program was fashioned the way Evans always does it: Seek the best advice possible, arrive at a remedy or course of action, build consensus, and get it enacted... Evans' approach to politics is exactly what Philadelphia needs: a willingness to transcend political and racial divides, to seek common ground, to find common solutions.

People often ask me whether I think this candidate or that candidate should be elected to public office. While every candidate and every situation is different, if there is one thing that I think all elected officials should have, it is a passion for making a difference. Truly great leaders – like Abraham Lincoln and LBJ – are driven by something more than a thirst for power and prestige. They are driven by a vision for how they want to make the world a better place. And they are driven by a belief that they can do that by working through the political process. Those are the people who we need to encourage to run for office, because those are the people who can and will make a difference.

After I lost the Appropriations Committee's chairmanship, everyone wanted to know what I would do next. To me, the answer to that question was simple. I would keep going to Harrisburg and advocating for legislation that would make Pennsylvania a stronger, more prosperous place. Beyond that, I don't know what my future holds. But I know that I will never stop looking for new ways and opportunities to make government more efficient. I will never stop fighting for the future.

Politics is a contact sport and if you play it long enough, you're bound to get hit. But despite the hits I've taken, I've never lost my faith in the process and my optimism for the future. Time and time again, I've seen how a group of active citizens can change the lives of a family and a community. Whether it is volunteering at a church or with a neighborhood association or with the local boys and girls club, we all have a part that we can play. The future is in our hands, and it is up to us to make the most of it.

INDEX

∞

Cߕ

CB

188

Made in the USA
Lexington, KY
22 December 2013